Time

in

Ezra Pound's

Work

TIME

IN

EZRA POUND'S

WORK

by William Harmon

THE UNIVERSITY OF NORTH CAROLINA PRESS
Chapel Hill

CONTENTS

PREFACE

"There is a TIME in these things," Ezra Pound says, contemplating events that take place at widely separated points in history. "It is quite obvious that we do not all of us inhabit the same time."[1]

From his earliest criticism to his last poems, such emphatic insistence on the importance of time animates all of his work. "The element most grossly omitted from treatises on harmony," he says, "is the element of TIME."[2] "Rhythm," he writes elsewhere, "is a form cut into TIME"; the sounds of the language "are the medium wherewith the poet cuts his design in TIME."[3] He demands that Thomas Jefferson be considered as an "agrarian IN the colonies and in the U.S.A. of HIS TIME,"[4] and he grants that "Goethe did attempt to do an honest job of work *in his time*."[5] An image, defined as "that which presents an intellectual and emotional complex in an instant of time," produces in the reader a "sense of freedom from time limits and space limits."[6] And in a fragment of his Canto CXV, first published when he was seventy-five years old, the poet reflects on his own career in time:

> *When one's friends hate each other*
> *how can there be peace in the world?*

> *Their asperities diverted me in my green time.*
> *A blown husk that is finished*
> > *but the light sings eternal*
> *a pale flare over marshes*
> > > *where the salt hay whispers to tide's change*
> *Time, space,*
> > *neither life nor death is the answer.*[7]

Pound's own work has often been analyzed in terms of time and timelessness. Wyndham Lewis, as we shall see, condemned Pound's obsession with the past; but other critics writing at about the same time arrived at conclusions very different from Lewis's. Dudley Fitts, perceptively reviewing *A Draft of XXX Cantos* in 1931, said, "The *Cantos* may be described as an epic of timelessness. That is to say, the poem represents Mr. Pound's endeavor to manage an arrest of time."[8] A few years later Yeats said of *The Cantos*, "There is no transmission through time, we pass without comment from ancient Greece to modern England, from modern England to medieval China; the symphony, the pattern, is timeless, flux eternal and without movement."[9]

More recent criticism has elaborated such notions. In one of his "Mayan Letters" (dated 8 March 1951), Charles Olson says:

Ez's epic solves problem by his ego: his single emotion breaks all down to his equals or inferiors (so far as I can see only two, possibly, are admitted, by him, to be his betters—Confucius, & Dante). Which assumption, that there are intelligent men whom he can outtalk, is beautiful because it destroys historical time, and thus creates the methodology of the Cantos, viz, a space-field where, by inversion, though the material is all time material, he has driven through it so sharply by the beak of his ego, that, he has turned time into what we must now have, space & its live air.[10]

Eva Hesse also finds something like the destruction of "historical time" in Pound's work. "For Pound," she says in a curious argument that begs the question once or twice, "it is not the past that has been moving towards us in linear progression, but he himself and his poem that move into the past. In line with modern scientific concepts, history for Pound is a space-time continuum, or a field of force. Thus time in the *Cantos* is not the objective, abstract and graduated time of calendar and clock that academic historical studies take for granted, but the subjective time of individual experience."[11] Similarly, Guy Davenport suggests a larger historical and philosophic context for Pound's struggle with time, and he restates the terms of Olson's analysis in a hyperbolic form that looks like the culmination of this species of criticism:

The placing of events in time is a romantic act; the *tremendum* is in the distance. There are no dates in the myths; from when to when did Heracles stride the earth? In a century obsessed with time, with archaeological dating, with the psychological recovery of time (Proust, Freud), Pound has written as if time were unreal, has, in fact, treated it as if it were space. . . . To say that *The Cantos* is a "voyage in time" is to be blind to the poem altogether. We miss immediately the achievement upon which the success of the poem depends, its rendering time transparent and negligible, its dismissing the supposed corridors and perspectives *down* which the historian invites us to look. Pound cancelled in his own mind the dissociations that had been isolating fact from fact for four centuries. . . . In Pound's spatial sense of time the past is here, now; its invisibility is our blindness, not its absence. The nineteenth century had put everything against the scale of time and discovered that all behaviour within time's monolinear progress was evolutionary. The past was a graveyard, a museum. It was Pound's determination to obliterate such a configuration of time and history, to treat what had become a world of ghosts as a world eternally present.[12]

My own formal work on Pound began in 1959 with a paper for a graduate course in modern criticism. For some years after that, at various schools, I continued the study, stimulated by Pound's work but disappointed by most critics. (The present work grows out of that course of study, for which I am deeply indebted to three teachers. Mr. Norman Maclean encouraged my initial speculations at the University of Chicago; Mr. Forrest Read supervised an M.A. thesis at the University of North Carolina, Chapel Hill; and Mr. Hugh Staples directed my Ph.D. work at the University of Cincinnati. To all three men—whom I now count as friends as well as teachers—I am most grateful.)

I found as I went along that time was indeed a central problem in the work of Pound, and I judged that some study remained to be carried out, even after D. D. Pearlman (*The Barb of Time*) and Hugh Kenner (*The Pound Era*) had published their findings. My notes cohered in a simple pattern of generic and chronological categories more or less causally arranged. I have placed a summary of aesthetic ideas about time in an appendix.

ACKNOWLEDGMENTS

To the Ellison Fund (University of Cincinnati) I am grateful for a generous fellowship that made an early version of this work possible. To the Smith Fund (University of North Carolina, Chapel Hill) I owe—and gladly deliver—thanks for aid in paying for secretarial help. Thanks are also due to Mrs. Muriel Dyer, Miss Susan DeFrancesco, and Mrs. Pamela Gurney, who accomplished various stages of the typing with exemplary dispatch. Messrs. C. Hugh Holman, Lewis Leary, and Louis D. Rubin, Jr., were good enough to read an earlier version of the manuscript and give me much advice and guidance.

ABBREVIATIONS

ABC *A B C of Reading*
ALS *A Lume Spento and Other Early Poems*
  C *The Cantos*
CSP *Collected Shorter Poems*
D&F *Drafts & Fragments of Cantos CX–CXVII*
 GB *Gaudier-Brzeska: A Memoir*
 GK *Guide to Kulchur*
 JM *Jefferson and/or Mussolini*
 LE *Literary Essays*
Ltrs *Letters, 1907–1914*
OED *Oxford English Dictionary*
 PM *Patria Mia*
 SR *The Spirit of Romance*

Time

in

Ezra Pound's

Work

1 POUND'S EARLIER CRITICAL WRITINGS ON CULTURAL TIME AND VALUE

For Ezra Pound, as for T. S. Eliot, the domain of poetry is the area where a general literary tradition meets the personal and social circumstances of an individual poet.[1] Poetry displays social backgrounds and honors social responsibilities: *The Cantos*, Pound says, is "the tale of the tribe,"[2] and one job of poetry, as Eliot suggests, is "to purify the dialect of the tribe."[3] To understand the context in which Pound's criticism and poetry are designed to operate, therefore, it is useful first to examine his ideas about culture, society, and history.

Needless to say, Pound was never a systematic political or social philosopher. Even when he was well into his fifties he could write in a letter to Santayana, "Premature to mention my 'philosophy,' call it a disposition. In another 30 years I may put the bits together, but probably won't."[4] This disposition, however inchoate, consistently led Pound to handle certain recurrent problems in certain characteristic ways. The unreality of historical time, for example, preoccupied him for decades. As early as 1910, in *The Spirit of*

Romance, he refuses to accept time as a circumstance that can limit the continuity of culture:

> It is dawn at Jerusalem while midnight hovers above the Pillars of Hercules. All ages are contemporaneous. It is B.C., let us say, in Morocco. The Middle Ages are in Russia. The future stirs already in the minds of the few. This is especially true of literature, where the real time is independent of the apparent, and where many dead men are our grandchildren's contemporaries, while many of our contemporaries have been already gathered into Abraham's bosom, or some more fitting receptacle.
>
> What we need is a literary scholarship, which will judge Theocritus and Yeats with one balance, and which will judge dead men as inexorably as dull writers of today, and will, with equity, give praise to beauty before referring to an almanack.[5]

It is a commonplace exaggeration, of course, to say that such powerful figures as Dante are "immortal" or, conversely, that some living man is effectively "dead." But Pound means more than that. Not only is Dante a living contemporary, unconfined by mortality, he is also not limited by the borders of his own personality; instead, he is "many men, and suffers as many" (*SR*, p. 177). These two radical concepts—the contemporaneity of culture and the continuity of personality—are keys to much of Pound's thought.

In "Histrion," one of his earliest poems, Pound presents the same ideas even more strongly, for here the poet's own personality is introduced; the idea of "the living Dante" is not a worn metaphor at all but an instance of something like metempsychosis:

> *No man hath dared to write this thing as yet,*
> *And yet I know, how that the souls of all men great*
> *At times pass through us,*
> *And we are melted into them, and are not*
> *Save reflexions of their souls.*
> *Thus am I Dante for a space and am*
> *One François Villon, ballad-lord and thief,*
> *Or am such holy ones I may not write*
> *Lest blasphemy be writ against my name;*
> *This for an instant and the flame is gone.*

> 'Tis as in midmost us there glows a sphere
> Translucent, molten gold, that is the "I"
> And into this some form projects itself:
> Christus, or John, or eke the Florentine;
> And as the clear space is not if a form's
> Imposed thereon,
> So cease we from all being for the time,
> And these, the Masters of the Soul, live on.[6]

This awkward poem, which was dropped from Pound's collections of verse after 1910,[7] is the most straightforward expression of his denial of the essential reality of both time and self. By the same creed he imagines a communal tradition that links certain extraordinary minds across space and time and permits the poet to conduct a running dialogue, not only with his contemporaries, but with his ancestors and descendants as well. In such a universe where events follow no necessary sequence, Pound can maneuver easily in patterns of anachronism. Villon, he says, "is a lurid canto of the *Inferno*, written too late to be included in the original text" (*SR*, p. 177). At times, when dealing with strictly historical matters, he gets tangled in his own vocabulary. He says, for example, "Adams lived to see an 'aristocracy of stock-jobbers and land-jobbers' in action and predicted them 'into time immemorial' (which phrase an ingenious grammarian *can* by great ingenuity catalogue and give a name to, by counting in a string of ellipses)."[8] By a similar procedure, something in Jefferson's writings "sounds almost like an echo of the Duce (hysteron proteron)."[9]

At this pole of the temporal axis, with all events potentially contemporaneous and all figures potentially coeval, Pound's own position is ambiguous. Although he lives in the present, he acts as a focus that gathers the spirits of "Masters of the Soul" and projects their image onto the future. He seems to be a vestige—a "man in love with the past"—and at the same time an antenna.[10] A poet who prizes order above all other values produces works that seem to be extremes of disorder; a critic who promotes renovation is stubbornly dedicated to repeating, often in deliberately archaic language, the triumphs of the past.

Two of Pound's closest associates, Wyndham Lewis and W. B. Yeats, tried to understand his relation to time and reached conclusions that could not be more divergent. To Lewis he was "the time-bound Ezra" and "a great *time-trotter*."[11] Lewis says, "Life is not his true concern, his gifts are all turned in the other direction. 'In his chosen or fated field he bows to no one,' to use his words. But his field is purely that of the *dead*. As the *nature mortist*, or painter essentially of still-life, deals for preference with life-that-is-still, that has not much life, so Ezra for preference consorts with the dead, whose life is preserved for us in books and pictures. He has never loved anything living as he has loved the dead."[12]

Richard Ellmann, tracing the changes in Yeats's attitude toward Pound in the characterological terms of *A Vision*, shows how pointedly Yeats's analysis of Pound's relation to time is opposed to Lewis's treatment of the same question. For Yeats, Pound is a man of "Phase 23," a placement explained by Ellmann: "Technical mastery offers the man of this phase his only refuge from masterless anarchy. Denying its subjective life, the mind delights only in the varied scene out the window, and seeks to construct a whole which is all event, all picture. Because of this submission to outwardness, the man of Phase 23 wishes to live in his exact moment of time as a matter of conscience, and, says Yeats, defends that moment like a theologian. He has in mind here Pound's imagist predilection, as well as his forever and dogmatically 'making it new.'"[13]

Since both Lewis and Yeats were considering Pound at roughly the same time (when he was in his thirties and forties), it seems odd that their judgments differ so greatly. Perhaps their ideas can be reconciled if Pound's relation to historical time is seen as a dialectical phenomenon with transcendent timelessness at one pole and immediate historical time at the other. If the extreme of timelessness is emphasized, Pound seems to be a man in love with everything but the present; if the extreme of immediate time is emphasized, he seems to be in love with nothing but the present.

Lewis and Yeats agree on two points, in any event. Pound is clearly in love with *something*, and, whatever its object, this love is realized in terms of time and timelessness.

Pound's belief that "all ages are contemporaneous" in no way diminishes his belief in the importance of careful attention to immediate experience. The integral side of his thought is balanced by the differential side. "The proper METHOD for studying poetry and good letters," he says, "is the method of contemporary biologists, that is careful first-hand examination of the matter, and continual COMPARISON of one 'slide' or specimen with another" (*ABC*, p. 17). A timeless idea exists only as manifest in a time-bound action; the temporal and spatial contingencies of an action are nearly as important as the unconditional idea that the action realizes. Pound's work as a whole can be seen as a powerfully sustained (but often frustrated) attempt to realize the ideals of beauty and order. The realization succeeds or suffers according to a variety of local and personal circumstances, and the ideals themselves undergo many metamorphoses.

I think one can distinguish a few major fluctuations in Pound's general attitude toward the possibility of realizing his ideals here and now. His goals, normally stated as "civilization" or "culture," are signalized by "public works" in both the civic and the aesthetic sense; correspondingly, the disintegration of the ideal is represented by images of ruin and fragmentation. I shall try to show that his early social thought begins with patriotic exuberance but turns during the First World War to a denial of the possibility of any general culture, and in the next chapter I shall examine a similar pattern of optimism and disappointment in his later writings.

The spirit of Romance is not only an ideal but also a zeitgeist and a spirit of certain related languages at a particular time. In *The Spirit of Romance*, Pound uses metaphors to describe how the spirit of art is realized in local materials. He says, "Art is a fluid moving above or over the minds of men. . . . Art or an art is not unlike a river, in that it is perturbed at times by the quality of the river bed, but is in a way independent of that bed. The color of the water depends upon the substance of the bed and banks immediate and preceding. Stationary objects are reflected, but the quality of motion is of the river. The scientist is concerned with all of these things, the artist with that which flows" (*SR*, pp. 7–8). Fluidity is again invoked toward the end of the book: "The spirit of the arts is dynamic. The arts are not passive, nor static, nor, in a sense, are they reflective, though reflection may assist at their birth" (*SR*, p. 222). Originally subtitled "An Attempt to Define Somewhat the Charm of the Pre-Renaissance Literature of Latin Europe," the book connects the literary arts of the past and the present by attempting "to examine certain forces, elements or qualities which were potent in the medieval literature of the Latin tongues, and are, I believe, still potent in our own" (*SR*, p. 7).

Pound met T. E. Hulme before the completion of *The Spirit of Romance*; it may be that he absorbed from Hulme the Bergsonian image of a fluid spirit of art interacting with static local conditions. Another spirit—a "sort of permanent basis in humanity" (*SR*, p. 92)—enables certain sensitive men to communicate with their predecessors and contemporaries by means of a kinship that Pound suggests in the essay "Psychology and the Troubadours" (published in 1912 and included in later editions of *The Spirit of Romance*):

Let us consider the body as pure mechanism. Our kinship to the ox we have constantly thrust upon us; but beneath this is our kinship to the vital universe, to the tree and the living rock, and because this is less obvious—and possibly more interesting—we forget it.

We have about us the universe of fluid force, and below us the germinal universe of wood alive, of stone alive. Man is—the sensitive physical part of him—a mechanism, for the purpose of our further discussion a mechanism rather like an electric appliance, switches, wires, etc. Chemically speaking, he is *ut credo*, a few buckets of water, tied up in a complicated sort of fig-leaf. As to his consciousness, the consciousness of some seems to rest, or to have its center more properly, in what the Greek psychologists called the *phantastikon*. Their minds are, that is, circumvolved about them like soap-bubbles reflecting sundry patches of the macrocosmos. And with certain others their consciousness is "germinal." Their thoughts are in them as the thought of the tree is in the seed, or in the grass, or the grain, or the blossom. And these minds are the more poetic, and they affect the mind about them, and transmute it as the seed the earth. And this latter sort of mind is close on the vital universe; and the strength of the Greek beauty rests in this, that it is ever at the interpretation of this vital universe, by its signs of gods and godly attendants and oreads.

[*SR*, pp. 92–93]

Here, in figures that suggest Coleridge as well as Bergson, is the condensed statement of the "disposition" that served the young Pound as ontology and epistemology and provided his poetry and criticism with one of their most durable problems. How does the essence of the world of ideal forms enter the existing world of real matter?

To the zeitgeist, which falls between the individual and the macrocosm, a writer can be attuned in a greater or lesser degree. The harmonious relation is partly a question of genre, according to Pound; so lyric poets and playwrights are less bound to their times than are writers of epic. Pound says, "Both Lope and Shakespeare add their incalculable selves to any expression of the Time Spirit; they owe much to it, but are not wholly dependent. Till now we have treated only of the generative forces in literature: Camoens is not a force, but a symptom. His work is utterly dependent upon the events and temper of his time; and in it, therefore, we may study that temper to advantage" (*SR*, pp. 214–15). Concerning the variable relation between genre and zeitgeist, Pound at an early age holds ideas that are clearly important to his own subsequent poetry: "An epic cannot be written against the grain of its time: the prophet or the satirist may hold himself aloof from his time, or run counter to it, but the writer of epos must voice the general heart. Although Camoens is undubitably a poet, one reads him today with a prose interest. *Os Lusiadas* is better than an historical novel; it gives us the tone of the time's thought. Thus far it is epic. By its very seeming faults it shows us what things interested the people of that time" (*SR*, p. 216).

In spite of the contemporaneity of culture and the continuity of personality, it remains important that certain writers lived at certain times. Writers like Dante and Shakespeare, "men 'born in their due time,'" will enjoy a success denied to such works as some "plays of Torres Naharro, born before their due time" (*SR*, pp. 111, 181).

A work can, of course, transcend its zeitgeist by embodying values of perennial concern. Claiming, for example, that the best of Lope de Vega's dramas are "as fresh and playable today as they were in 1600," Pound is led into one of his characteristic *hysteron-proteron* positions. The proof of the durability of Lope's comedies, he says, is to be found in a play like *El Desprecio Agradecido*, "which might have been written—bar certain vagaries of chronos—by Shaw in collaboration with Joachim du Bellay" (*SR*, p. 197). Moreover, it is possible for a work to transcend its age not by moving up toward celestial virtues but rather by moving down toward irreducible human facts. Pound says, "If Dante reaches out of his time, and by rising above it escapes many of its limitations, Villon in some way speaks below the voice of his age's convention, and thereby outlasts it. He is utterly mediaeval, yet his poems mark the end of mediaeval literature. Dante strives constantly for a nobler state on earth. His aspiration separates him from his time, and the ordinary reader from his work" (*SR*, pp. 170–71).

According to *The Spirit of Romance*, then, each age is distinguished by a governing spirit that is a function of time, place, language, and other immediate circumstances. It is possible for a writer who is in complete accord with this spirit to reflect it, particularly in epic. A writer like Dante, whose values reach beyond those of his age, can register his thought best in a quasi-lyric drama of epic scope (*SR*, pp. 153–54); on the other hand, a writer like Villon—whose values, being simply and fundamentally human, are below those of his age—can work best in personal lyrics.

In this problematic area where the zeitgeist meets the individual talent, an obvious case in point is Walt Whitman. In fact, *The Americanness of Walt Whitman*, alongside such other volumes as *The Great Tariff Debate: 1820–1830* and *The Pullman Boycott of 1894*, is one volume in a series called *Problems in American Civilization*.[14] In 1909, when his thinking about literature was strongly directed toward such issues as the connection between poet and zeitgeist, Pound set down a brief testament called "What I Feel about Walt Whitman." He was twenty-three years old (as his spelling may indicate) and had just begun his residence in London:

From this side of the Atlantic I am for the first time able to read Whitman, and from the vantage of my education and—if it be permitted a man of my scant years—my world citizenship: I see him America's poet. The only Poet before the artists of the Carman-Hovey period, or better, the only one of the conventionaly recognized "American Poets" who is worth reading.

He *is* America. His crudity is an exceding great stench, but it *is* America. He is the hollow place in the rock that echos with his time. He *does* "chant the crucial stage" and he is the "voice triumphant." He is disgusting. He is an excedingly nauseating pill, but he acomplishes his mission.[15]

Having identified Whitman with America, he next identifies himself with Whitman:

Mentaly I am a Walt Whitman who has learned to wear a colar and a dress shirt (although at times inimical to both). Personaly I might be very glad to conceal my relationship to my spiritual father and brag about my more congenial ancestry—Dante, Shakespeare, Theocritus, Villon, but the descent is a bit difficult to establish. And, to be frank, Whitman is to my fatherland (Patriam quam odi et amo for no uncertain reasons) what Dante is to Italy and I at my best can only be a strife for a renaissance in America of all the lost or temporarily mislaid beauty, truth, valor, glory of Greece, Italy, England and all the rest of it.[16]

It would not be very surprising to hear Whitman say, "Der Zeitgeist, c'est moi"—or, at any rate, to hear such a claim entered in his behalf by another thoroughgoingly American polyglot-poet. Pound's lover's quarrel with his country could be traced on the same line of his graph as his quarrel with Whitman. Pound says, "I am (in common with every educated man) an heir of the ages and I demand my birth-right. Yet if Whitman represented his time in language acceptable to one accustomed to my standard of intellectual-artistic living he would belie his time and nation. And yet I am but one of his 'ages and ages' encrustations' or to be exact an encrustation of the next age. The vital part of my message, taken from the sap and fibre of America, is the same as his."[17]

Pound also says of Whitman, "I read him (in many parts) with acute pain, but when I write of certain things I find myself using his rythms. The expression of certain things related to cosmic consciousness seems tainted with this maramis."[18] In *The Spirit of*

Romance, which was published a year after these words were written, Pound seems to be attacking (and quoting) his own earlier ideas on the matter of Whitman's cosmic vision: "The disciples of Whitman cry out concerning the 'cosmic sense' but Whitman, with all his catalogues and flounderings, has never so perfectly expressed the perception of cosmic consciousness as does Dante (in *Paradiso* I. 68–69)" (*SR*, p. 155). He even attempts to parody Whitman, with clumsy results:

> *Lo, behold, I eat water-melons. When I eat water-melons*
> *   the world eats water-melons through me.*
> *When the world eats water-melons, I partake of the*
> *   world's water-melons.*

[*SR*, p. 168]

A few years later, in "A Pact," he arrived at a compromise with his old "spiritual father":

> *I make a pact with you, Walt Whitman—*
> *I have detested you long enough.* [19]

Pound's quarrel with Whitman and America continues in *Patria Mia*, a little book written "prior to 1913" but not published until 1950.[20] Here Pound says, "Now Whitman was not an artist, but a reflex, the first honest reflex, in an age of papier mache letters. He was the time and the people (of 1860–80); that is, perhaps, as offensive as anything one can say of either" (*PM*, p. 38). Having said, "I trust in the national chemical, or, if the reader be of Victorian sensibility, let us say the 'spirit' or the 'temper' of the nation" (*PM*, p. 62), he proceeds to examine the "American keynote":

It is, as nearly as I can define it, a certain generosity; a certain carelessness, or looseness, if you will; a hatred of the sordid, an ability to forget the part for the sake of the whole, a desire for largeness; a willingness to stand exposed.

> "*Camerado, this is no book;*
> *Who touches this touches a man.*"

The artist is ready to endure personally a strain which his craftsmanship would scarcely endure.

Here is a spirit, one might say, as hostile to the arts as was the Anglo-Saxon objection to speaking at all.

Yet the strength of both peoples is just here; that one undertakes to keep quiet until there is something worth saying, and the other will undertake nothing in its art for which it will not be in person responsible.

One reason why Whitman's reception in America has been so tardy is that he says so many things which we are accustomed, almost unconsciously, to take for granted. He was so near the national colour that the nation hardly perceived him against that background. He came at a time when America was proud of a few deeds and of a few principles. He came before the nation was self-conscious or introspective or subjective; before the nation was interested in being itself.

The nation has no interest in seeing its face in the glass. It wanted a tradition like other nations, and it got Longfellow's "Tales of a Wayside Inn" and "Hiawatha" and "Evangeline."

Whitman established the national *timbre*. One may not need him at home. It is in the air, this tonic of his. But if one is abroad; if one is ever likely to forget one's birth-right, to lose faith, being surrounded by disparagers, one can find, in Whitman, the reassurance. Whitman goes bail for the nation.

[*PM*, pp. 62–64]

Since Pound explicitly identifies Whitman with the American national character (or spirit, chemical, temper, *timbre*, or grain) at a given time, his remarks on Whitman make up a convenient paradigm of his general thought regarding race and zeitgeist. There were, to be sure, occasions when his viewpoint grew less parochial and more ecumenical. In late 1913, for example, he wrote to Harriet Monroe, "Until 'we' accept what I've been insisting on for a decade, i.e., a universal standard which pays no attention to time or country—a Weltlitteratur standard—there is no hope" (*Ltrs*, pp. 24–25). But in *Patria Mia* the emphasis is very much on a particular time and country. He vigorously attacks the country's shortcomings, particularly in education and the arts, but he has hope. "The thesis I defend is: that America has a chance for a Renaissance and that certain absurdities in the manners of American action are, after all, things of the surface and not of necessity the symptoms of sterility or even of fatal disease" (*PM*, p. 24). Brought up in the "American mediaeval system," he sees a sign of impending rebirth in the mass of humanity in New York City, "a crowd pagan as ever imperial Rome was, eager, careless, with an animal vigour unlike that of any European crowd that I have ever looked at." He says that, compared to New York, Venice "seems like a tawdry scene in a play-house"; and "when Mr. Marinetti and his friends shall have succeeded in destroying that ancient city, we will rebuild Venice on the Jersey mud flats and use the same for a tea-shop" (*PM*, pp. 26, 33).

Having set down his "belief in the imminence of an American Risorgimento" (*PM*, p. 41), Pound then comes forward as a practical Yankee who does not dream idly. He offers a program for the realization of a new society, based chiefly on increased financial support for artists. Concentrating on the American qualities of exuberance and wealth, he is led again into a burlesque of Whitman:

> Yet American taste and discrimination will be held ridiculous in the world's eyes until America learns to pay reverence to something better. And for that matter America has learned. I should write "Until America learns to *limit* her reverence to something a cut above"—"I hear America a-singing."
>
> > *"Fat, sleek, contented with emotions well*
> > *Below the diaphragm."*
>
> [*PM*, p. 38]

Harriet Monroe was starting *Poetry* magazine at about the same time that Pound was writing *Patria Mia*, and he welcomed her undertaking as a sign of the improvement in American taste. He wrote to her, "Any agonizing that tends to hurry what I believe in the end to be inevitable, our American Risorgimento, is dear to me. That awakening will make the Italian Renaissance look like a tempest in a teapot! The force we have, and the impulse, but the guiding sense, the discrimination in applying the force, we must wait and strive for" (*Ltrs*, p. 10).

Some of the ideas from the temporarily lost *Patria Mia* were salvaged for use in an article called "The Renaissance" that appeared in three installments in *Poetry* just at the outbreak of the First World War. Unlike *Patria Mia*, however, this article seems to be written by a comfortably naturalized world citizen who is offering avuncular counsel to a country that is no longer quite his own. Calling for "a criticism of poetry based on world-poetry, on the work of maximum excellence,"[21] Pound now considers Whitman only a forerunner and not a great exemplar who could contribute to the "palette" of literary possibilities: "No American poetry is of any use for the palette. Whitman is the best of it, but he never pretended to have reached the goal. He knew himself, and proclaimed himself 'a start in the right direction.' He never said, 'American poetry is to stay where I left it'; he said it was to go on from where he started it" (*LE*, p. 218).[22] After quoting Henry James on the absence of art and letters in America, Pound continues, "And yet we look to the dawn, we count up our symptoms; year in and year out we say we have this and that, we have so much, and so much. Our best asset is a thing of the spirit" (*LE*, pp. 218–19). And in the second and third parts of "The Renaissance," he repeats the call of *Patria Mia* for communities of artists supported by patrons and the government.

A comparison of *Patria Mia* and "The Renaissance" discloses a subtle but definite shift in Pound's attitude toward developments in historical time. In *Patria Mia* he repeats the idea of contemporaneous ages, first expressed in *The Spirit of Romance*, and suggests that the "mediaeval" period in America could be succeeded by a renaissance—events parallel to those in the history of Italy—if only the artistic and financial resources be marshaled correctly. In "The Renaissance," on the other hand, the emphasis is not on life cycles manifest in separate but parallel cultures but rather on a continuity of world culture in which any country may participate. The specific American spirit is minimized, the significance of the zeitgeist is diminished, and the importance of Whitman as avatar and "spiritual father" is conspicuously reduced.

Between 1915 and 1920 Pound's preoccupation with the meaning of cultural and historical time is still very much in evidence, but there is an equally evident erosion of his original spirit of patriotic optimism. Henry James, for whom Pound felt the greatest respect, died in 1916, and some of Pound's close friends—including T. E.

Hulme and the sculptor Henri Gaudier-Brzeska—were killed in the war. He seems to have given up on *Poetry* as an organ of the American *Risorgimento*, and his prose deals more with technical and formal criticism and less with cultural history. His tone becomes humorlessly impatient, as in "The Constant Preaching to the Mob" (June 1916), in which he defends the vigor and depth of Anglo-Saxon elegiac verse against critics who consider it merely "entertainment": "Time and again the old lie. There is no use talking to the ignorant about lies, for they have no criteria. Deceiving the ignorant is by some regarded as evil, but it is the demagogue's business to bolster up his position and to show that God's noblest work is the demagogue" (*LE*, p. 64). In a September 1916 letter to Mencken, he says that "the *country* U.S.A. is hopeless and may as well go to hell its own way. Hell is a place completely paved with Billy Sunday and Ellis" (*Ltrs*, p. 97).[23] A year later, in a letter to William Carlos Williams, he again associates hell with America: "I note your invitation to return to my fatherland (pencil at the top of your letter sic. g. t. h.); I shall probably accept it at the end of the war" (*Ltrs*, p. 123). Other parts of this letter are also interesting:

And America! What the hell do you a bloomin' foreigner know about the place? Your père only penetrated the edge, and you've never been west of Upper Darby, or the Maunchunk switchback. Would Harriet, with the swirl of prairie wind in her underwear, or the virile Sandburg recognize you, an effete Easterner, as a REAL American? INCONCEIVABLE!!!. . .

The thing that saves your work is *opacity*, and don't you forget it. Opacity is NOT an American quality. Fizz, swish, gabble of verbiage, these are echt Amerikanisch.

(*Ltrs*, pp. 123–24)

And in another letter to Mencken, written in March 1918, he snipes at Whitman once again (in explaining why Eliot had published his *Ezra Pound, His Metric and Poetry* anonymously): "I had just boomed Eliot, but he was the only person one could trust NOT to talk about the Rocky Mountains, the bold unfettered West, the Kawsmos etc." (*Ltrs*, p. 132).

The August 1918 number of the *Little Review*, a special issue on the work of Henry James, contains a very interesting essay by

Eliot[24] and a long study by Pound that calls itself "a Baedecker to a continent" (*LE*, p. 295). That is a most engaging figure of speech. Whereas Whitman himself had *been* America for Pound in 1909, James's work is described here as a continent in its own right—a geographical mass that an enthusiast could set against the American fatherland, called earlier "almost a continent and hardly yet a nation" (*PM*, p. 21). The work of James is, in effect, America's "anti-self,"[25] a large continent of cultural achievement in contrast to the "hopeless" country whose positive self is concentrated in Whitman. Pound's essay gives some idea of what his thought was like during the First World War, when he was at the height of both his indignation against the American culture and his admiration for the man whom he had considered "the greatest living American" (*LE*, p. 218).[26] He now praises James in terms very much like those in which he had praised Whitman in *Patria Mia*:

In his presentation of America he is greatly attentive, and, save for the people in *Coeur Simple*, I doubt if any writer has done more of "this sort of thing" for his country, this portrayal of the typical thing in timbre and quality—balanced, of course, by the array of spittoons in the Capitol (*The Point of View*).

Still if one is seeking a Spiritual Fatherland, if one feels the exposure of what he would not have scrupled to call, two clauses later, such a windshield, *The American Scene* greatly provides it.

[*LE*, p. 303]

Whitman, then, Pound's "spiritual father" in 1909, has been the country for the young poet. By 1918, however, the function of the "Spiritual Fatherland" has been taken over by the work of James, in which one finds the country created anew. "I think half the American idiom is recorded in Henry James' writing," Pound says; "and whole decades of American life that otherwise would have been utterly lost, wasted, rotting in the unhermetic jars of bad writing, of inaccurate writing" are there preserved (*LE*, p. 296). His highest praise goes to James's nonfiction:

The American Scene, triumph of the author's long practice. A creation of America. A book no "serious American" will neglect. How many Americans make any attempt toward a realization of that country is of course beyond our power to compute. The desire to see the national face in a mirror may be in itself an exotic. I know of no such grave record, of no such attempt at faithful portrayal as *The American Scene*. . . . There is nothing to be gained by making excerpts; the volume is large, but one should in time drift through it. I mean any American with pretences to an intellectual life should drift through it. It is not enough to have perused "The Constitution" and to have "heerd tell" of the national founders.

[*LE*, p. 327]

Writing to Marianne Moore in 1919, Pound interrupts a discussion of American culture to say, "Must let it alone (I must). Must return to the unconcern with U.S.A. that I had before 1911–12" (*Ltrs*, p. 148). In the next year, provoked by an attack in Williams's *Kora in Hell*, he writes his most sustained meditation on the state of culture in Europe and America in the immediately postwar period. In three letters written to Williams on 11 and 12 September 1920, he expresses his dismay at the charge in *Kora in Hell* that he had been "the best enemy United States verse has."[27] The first of these letters ends with Pound's admission that he simply does not know what to do with himself:

AND now that there is no longer any intellectual *life* in England save what centres in this eight by ten pentagonal room, now that Rémy and Henry are gone and Yeats faded, and NO literary publication whatever extant in England, save what "we" print (*Egoist* and Ovid Press), the question remains whether I have to give up every shred of comfort, every scrap of my personal life, and "gravitate" to a New York which wants me as little now as it did ten and fifteen years ago. Whether, from the medical point of view it is masochism for me even to stay here, instead of shifting to Paris. Whether self-inflicted torture ever has the slightest element of dignity in it?

Or whether I am Omar.

Have I a country at all . . . now that Mouquin is no more, and that your father has no more goldwasser, and the goldwasser no obescent bonhommes to pour it out for me?

Or you who sees no alternative?

[*Ltrs*, pp. 158–59][28]

"Have I a country at all?"—the question takes us back to Pound's idea in *The Spirit of Romance* that Villon is the type of general suffering humanity without any of the specific distinguishing coloration of his social conditions. Villon, who "in some way speaks below the voice of his age's conventions, and thereby outlasts it" (*SR*, p. 170), is mentioned again at the end of *Patria Mia*, where Pound is arguing for subsidies for artists. A man too low on the social scale to be affected by nationality or zeitgeist, he represents the artist who is given no support by his society: "Villon is the stock example of those who advocate the starvation of artists, but the crux is here, to wit, that Villon had nothing whatsoever to gain by producing a bastard art. No harpies besought him for smooth optimism, for patriotic sentiment, and for poems 'to suit the taste of our readers.' If he had nothing to lose by one sort of writing he had equally little to gain by any other" (*PM*, p. 97).

Remy de Gourmont is another figure who concentrated Pound's earlier social thought. Whitman and James were self and antiself of America, and Villon and Dante were, respectively, below and above the spirit of their time; Gourmont's position is indifference to all external circumstances. His attitude, conditionally endorsed by Pound, is expressed in one sentence: "Or un écrivain, un poète, un philosophe, un homme des régions intellectuelles n'a qu'une patrie: sa langue."[29]

Pound's "Rémy de Gourmont: A Distinction, Followed by Notes" appeared in the *Little Review* early in 1919, four years after Gourmont's death. The "distinction" that Pound has in mind is quite pointed: "The mind of Rémy de Gourmont was less like the mind of Henry James than any contemporary mind I can think of" (*LE*, p. 339). In contrast to James, who "was concerned with mental temperatures, circumvolvulous social pressures, the clash of contending conventions," Gourmont "was an artist of the nude. He was an intelligence almost more than an artist; when he portrays, he is concerned with hardly more than the permanent human elements. His people are only by accident of any particular era. He is poet, more by possessing a certain quality of mind than by virtue of having written fine poems; you could scarcely contend that he was a novelist" (*LE*, pp. 339–40).

Pound then makes a crucial equation that stands at the opposite pole from "Whitman *is* America" and shows how much his thinking changed from 1909 to 1919. He says, "There are plenty of people who do not know what the civilized mind is like, just as there were plenty of mules in England who did not read Landor contemporaneously, or who did not in his day read Montaigne. Civilization is individual" (*LE*, p. 344). Clearly, then, the business of a writer who "n'a qu'une patrie: sa langue" is not to write a book called *Patria Mia* or to prophesy that an American Renaissance is coming that will make Italy's look like a tempest in a teapot. For Gourmont, all collective loyalties—"Famille, Patrie, Etat, Société, etc."—were nothing more than "un groupe de métaphores," and the statutes of aesthetic law were correspondingly revised: "Le crime capital pour écrivain, c'est le conformisme, l'imitativité, la soumission aux règles et aux enseignements."[30] Gourmont's philosophy is summed up by Pound in five sentences: "Christianity lends itself to fanaticism. Barbarian ethics proceed by general taboos. The relation of two individuals is so complex that no third person can pass judgment upon it. Civilization is individual. The truth is the individual" (*LE*, p. 355).

Beginning with the outbreak of the First World War, Pound comes more and more to exemplify such Gourmontian attitudes; his criticism stresses individual values over social commitments and his more general comments on European life stress individual civilization as the most reliable instrument of benevolence.

Reviewing *Dubliners* in 1914, he says, "Good writing, good presentation can be specifically local, but it must not depend on locality. Mr. Joyce does not present 'types' but individuals. I mean he deals with common emotions which run through all races. . . . He is classic in that he deals with normal things and with normal people."[31] In 1917 he compares *Prufrock and Other Observations* to *A Portrait of the Artist as a Young Man*: "James Joyce has written the best novel of my decade, and perhaps the best criticism of it has come from a Belgian who said, 'All this is as true of my country as of Ireland.' Eliot has a like ubiquity of application. Art does not avoid universals, it strikes at them all the harder in that it strikes through particulars" (*LE*, p. 420). And in 1922 he uses the same standard and much the same language to praise *Ulysses* and its author: "He has presented Ireland under British domination, a picture so veridic that a ninth rate coward like Shaw (Geo. B.) dare not even look it in the face. By extension he has presented the whole occident under the domination of capital. The details of the street map are local but Leopold Bloom (*né Virag*) is ubiquitous" (*LE*, p. 407).

Whitman spoke of the spirit of 1776 as "the haughty defiance of the Year One."[32] In a similar fashion Pound took 30 October 1921 —his thirty-sixth birthday and the date of the completion of *Ulysses*—as the starting point of a new age. A peculiar calendar printed in the *Little Review* (Spring 1922) marked the end of the Christian era and the beginning of the "YEAR 1 p. s. U."[33] Pound at this period speaks of the twentieth century as the "first of the new era" (*LE*, p. 408); and in "James Joyce et Pécuchet," published in June 1922 in the *Mercure de France*, he calls "l'année du centenaire de Flaubert" (which began in 1921) the "première d'une ère nouvelle."[34]

With the dawning of this new era, Pound seems to have rid himself of his depressing feelings of statelessness and isolation. As a very young man he had subscribed to the idea of an enveloping and determining zeitgeist, but within a few years he began to think of writers more as individual creators than as passive instruments of their circumstances. Earlier he had vainly tried to promote the public institution of foundations to support the arts. During the First World War he concentrated less on grandiose formal schemes and more on getting some help from individual or public funds for certain artists who were in need. He managed to have Joyce receive seventy-five pounds from the Royal Literary Fund,[35] for example, and he was busy putting artists into contact with editors, patrons, and employers. By the beginning of his new era of individual civilization in the early 1920s, however, he largely gave up on patrons and foundations, because whatever support he could arrange from such sources was gained only at the sacrifice of many hours spent writing letters and correcting misconceptions—another variety of the distasteful preaching to, and pleading with, the mob.

The "Bel Esprit" project of 1922 represents Pound's new attitude of embattled artistic isolation and individualism. This was a scheme by which artists themselves would pledge a fairly small amount to a fund to be used to support some single artist. Pound's outline of the project sounds again the Gourmontian note of denial of such collective "metaphors" as state, culture, and society:

> There is no organized or coordinated civilization left, only individual scattered survivors.
>
> Aristocracy is gone, its function was to select.
>
> Only those of us who know what civilization is, only those of us who want better literature, better art, not more art, can be expected to pay for it. No use waiting for masses to develop a finer taste, they aren't moving that way. . . .
>
> Darkness and confusion as in Middle Ages; no chance of general order or justice; we can only release an individual here or there. . . .
>
> Must restart civilization; people who say they care, DON'T care unless they care to the extent of £5 in the spring and £5 in autumn, ridiculous to say they do, if they won't run to that, can't expect a civilization.
>
> [*Ltrs*, pp. 172–73]

"Bel Esprit" raised some money for Eliot, who received an award from the *Dial* at about the same time, but the good-natured undertaking did not endure to assist any other artists.[36]

Pound's belief in a new era of individual civilization confirmed his acceptance of his own condition of exile and statelessness. In 1924 he described the general "republic of letters" as a kind of real country, much in the same way that, six years earlier, he had treated the work of Henry James as a "continent." Writing on the award of the Nobel Prize for 1923 to Yeats, Pound says that if "the award had not gone to Yeats it might well have gone to another Irishman, and if it can not, for some national reason, go for two consecutive years to the same nation, one might nominate James Joyce as representative of the republic of letters, or of the Heimatlos; who are, at this moment, as respectable a collection of writers as is found in any one country."[37]

But Pound's status as a civilized individual owing allegiance only to the country of the *Heimatlos* did not harmonize with his fundamental impulse toward generously benevolent social action. "The curse of me & my nation," he said in a letter to Joyce in 1920, "is that we always think things can be bettered by immediate action of some sort, *any* sort rather than no sort."[38] He had moved from London to Paris in the early 1920s. By 1925, when he was settled in Italy, Hemingway wrote of him, "As he takes no interest in Italian politics and does not mind Italian cookery he may stay there some time."[39] But Pound, as we know now, was beginning to take a very great deal of interest in Italian politics. Instead of living out his chosen life of exile from America in Gourmontian indifference to social affairs, he plunged into a prolonged examination of collective civilization in Italy and America.[40] This undertaking, which had such unhappy results for Pound personally, marks the beginning of the second major cycle in the development of his social thought about the meaning of time and culture.

POUND'S LATER CRITICAL WRITINGS ON CULTURAL TIME AND VALUE

2

Mussolini came to power on 30 October 1922—on Pound's thirty-seventh birthday and, according to the *"Little Review* Calendar," the beginning of the second year of a new era. A new calendar using Roman numerals followed by "Era Fascista" was introduced in Italy; in time Pound himself began to follow this style of reckoning. By saying "the dawn of the year XII of the present era," he located the "Date Line" of his *Make It New*,[1] and soon such terms as "dodicesimo anno E. F.," "anno seidici," and "anno sixteen" began to appear in *The Cantos*.[2]

Pound's association with political developments between 1920 and 1945 is, of course, more than a matter of calendars, but a very important element in his social thought is his concern with putting timeless values into action in a timely fashion and in harmony with the spirit of a particular time and place. Two of the books that he wrote in the 1930s, *Jefferson and/or Mussolini* and *Guide to Kulchur*, show very different applications of his thought about time and the times.

According to a foreword signed "E. P., Rapallo, April, XIII,"

Jefferson and/or Mussolini was written in 1933 and was then re-jected by forty publishers.[3] It is easy to sympathize with their point of view, for the book seldom rises above a very low level of clum-sily executed name-calling. The book so lacks clear phrase and design that it cannot be summarized fairly. One can only point out certain salient features and try to relate them to what Pound says elsewhere.

The title *Jefferson and/or Mussolini* states the question in terms of individual political figures, and throughout the book ideology as such is subordinate to other concerns. The Pound of 1933 seems willing to accept any leader—Mussolini or Lenin, Napoleon or Jefferson—as long as timely measures are implemented to put ideals of social order into action. Pound praises Mussolini for the usual reasons: he managed to get the Italian trains running on time and he drained some marshes. Having witnessed such achieve-ment, Pound is willing to sacrifice almost any principle of political behavior for the sake of efficient public works and services. Mus-solini's dictatorial concentration of power, his censorship of news-papers, his one-party rule, his ad hoc making and breaking of laws, and his embargo on emigration are all justified by Pound because these policies—like some adopted by Jefferson—are needed to solve immediate problems.

As early as *Patria Mia* Pound declares himself an "opportunist," meaning in that context that he is willing to accept practically any form of government, without regard to its principles, as long as it fosters the arts.[4] And in *Jefferson and/or Mussolini* he says, "There is opportunism and opportunism. The word has a bad meaning because in a world of Metternichs, and Talleyrands it means doing the other guy the minute you get the chance" (*JM*, p. 15). A little later he explains the difference: "To cut the cackle, you can have an OPPORTUNIST who is RIGHT, that is who has certain convictions and who drives them through circumstance, or batters and forms circumstance with them" (*JM*, pp. 17–18). It is not clear whether Pound means by *opportunism* the sacrifice of principle to immediate needs or the sacrifice of due process of law and other incidental machinery of government to the working out, by any means, of some general conviction. He says, "Jefferson was denounced as vacillating. A man who plugs after a main purpose for sixty years is no more vacillating than a general who wins a campaign by keeping his light troops mobile. Opportunist? Rightly opportunist!" (*JM*, p. 64) But a metaphor and an exclamation point do nothing to clarify the question, for the only principle served by any sort of opportunism is the principle of letting the needs of a certain problem in a limited time and place override the preservation of timeless principles.

In *The Spirit of Romance*, Pound praises a dynamic, fluid kind of consciousness "close on the vital universe," a poetic imagination found in men whose thought is not mechanical but "germinal." He says, "Their thoughts are in them as the thought of the tree is in the seed, or in the grass, or the grain, or the blossom. And these minds are the more poetic, and they affect mind about them, and transmute it as the seed the earth."[5] This idea has obvious political applications; the figure of germination is revived in *Jefferson and/or Mussolini* to rationalize Jefferson's ostensible lack of permanent principles:

> The modern American cheap sneers at democracy and at some of Jefferson's slogans are based on the assumption that Jefferson's ideas were *idées fixes*.
>
> Attacks on Jefferson's sincerity made during his lifetime were made by the same type of idiot, on precisely the opposite tack. I mean because they weren't *idées fixes*, and because Jefferson was incapable of just that form of stupidity.
>
> An *idée fixe* is a dead, stiff, varnished "idea" existing in a vacuum.
>
> The ideas of genius, or of "men of intelligence" are organic and germinal, the "seed" of the scriptures.
>
> You put one of these ideas somewhere, i.e. somewhere in a definite space and time, and something begins to happen.
>
> [*JM*, p. 21]

Jefferson and/or Mussolini itself invites the same criticisms, however idiotic they may have seemed to Pound. Improvising tactics and principles as he goes along, Pound vacillates between the condemnation of permanent values as dead, fixed ideas and the elevation of them to the status of eternal realities. He noisily espouses

"ORDER" (*JM*, p. 128) in a book that is endlessly imprecise and disorderly, presumably excusing the slovenliness as the faithful tracing of a germinal mind in action. The paradox is tragic. It seems that Pound had been seeking repose after many years of bitterly frustrating personal effort in America, England, and France. The recognition and support that he had won for himself and some of his superlatively gifted associates were achieved only at a very high cost in time, energy, and patience. At the age of forty he moved to a small town on the Italian Riviera, apparently without giving much consideration to the prevailing form of government. He soon found himself in the presence of a comprehensive campaign of political reform led by an articulate dictator only two years older than himself, and he must have been delighted, after years of struggle against ignorance and mismanagement, to see rail schedules followed and marshes drained and unemployment reduced.

It is not hard to understand the motives behind *Jefferson and/or Mussolini* when one tries to imagine a man of Pound's talent and sensitivity being exposed to the inanities that he found in America and England and then, by a powerful turn of luck, realizing that he was in the midst of a dynamic revolution that in spite of certain unattractive characteristics seemed dedicated to the heroic restoration of order in Italy. But his willingness to excuse Mussolini's cruelties and excesses remains a source of dismay to many sympathizers. In the arts Pound was one of the most discerning critics of the twentieth century; he recognized immediately the merit of Joyce, Eliot, Frost, Lawrence, Williams, and Hemingway, and he was just as quick in dismissing inferior artists. But those punctual locomotives and drained marshes warped his judgment and reduced him for a while to the advocacy of expediency and bombast. It should be remembered that *Jefferson and/or Mussolini* was hastily written in early 1933, when Hitler, who had just come to power in Germany, seemed to many people more a sideshow than a threat to civilization. It was also before Italy invaded Ethiopia, annexed Albania, and intervened in the Spanish Civil War. But even in the context of 1933—even, indeed, in the pages of *Jefferson and/or Mussolini* itself—there is plentiful evidence of Mussolini's pernicious misuse of power within his own country. But Pound simply ignores the issues and indulges in ugly name-calling. In the month before Franklin Roosevelt took office, for example, he was already being dismissed by Pound as a "weak sister" merely on the basis of something that Mencken happened to say in a letter (*JM*, pp. x, 103).

The subtitle "L'Idea Statale: Fascism as I Have Seen It" contains the kernel of the dilemma that wrecks *Jefferson and/or Mussolini*. Pound wants to discuss an *idea*, but he can approach the idea only through its realization in action. He says, "Let us deny that *real* intelligence exists until it comes into action" (*JM*, p. 18). In Gourmont's criticism the very idea of an "idea" is relegated, as we have seen, to the same midden of rhetorical metaphors that holds Society, Nation, and Family. Pound needs to dissociate *l'idea statale* from such a taint, and he struggles to distinguish the idea *in vacuo* from the idea in action. He says, "A man in desperate circumstances, let us say, Remy de Gourmont in pre-war France might get to the point of thinking that an idea is spoiled by being brought into action, but Gourmont also got to the point of cursing intelligence altogether. . . . He then got round to defining intellect as the fumbling about in the attempt to create instinct, or at any rate on the road towards instinct. And his word instinct came to mean merely PERFECT and complete intelligence *with a limited scope* applied to recurrent conditions" (*JM*, p. 18).

Here, swamped in philosophical difficulties, Pound is clearly beyond his depth; he never settles down with an idea that can accommodate both the "permanent human elements" (which he had praised as Gourmont's primary subject[6]) and the local shaping and coloring that abstract concepts take on as they pass into a field of action. Looking for a way to excuse Mussolini's patent disregard for democratic principles, Pound abandons the notion of individual civilization that he took from Gourmont and reverts to a racially and temporally oriented concept of "national character" rather like the ideas expressed in *The Spirit of Romance* and *Patria Mia*.

No longer can he claim membership in the scattered *patria* of the *Heimatlos*, for he must invoke an ineluctable historical process at work among specific Italian conditions with which he is personally familiar. Opportunism is geared to local conditions, so that principles can be shelved, according to Pound, with no danger of their being diminished or forgotten. Since the ultimate value of *l'idea statale* is quite beyond proof, Pound must add to his subtitle the clause "as I have seen it." Just as a policy in the abstract is beyond proof, his argument for the policy in action as he has seen it is beyond refutation, at least to the extent that one is willing to accept Pound as a competent witness. According to an old maxim, the wise lawyer argues the law when his facts are weak and argues the facts when his law is weak. That is what Pound does in *Jefferson and/or Mussolini*. He elects the option—to argue principles or particulars—that best serves his journalistic purpose. He says, "No American who hasn't lived for years in Italy has the faintest shade of a shadow of a conception of the multiformity and diversity of wholly separate and distinct conservatisms that exist in this country" (*JM*, p. 32). By these terms the force of peculiar local circumstances is absolute; but by the same terms the principles behind the particular policy in use can never be transferred to any other circumstances. The radical flaw of the book lies in Pound's failure to reconcile the terms *idea* and *action*.

Early in the book he says, "I don't propose to limit my analysis to what Tom Jefferson recommended *in a particular time and place*. I am concerned with what he actually did, with the way his mind worked both when faced with a particular problem *in* a particular geography, and when faced with the unending problem of CHANGE" (*JM*, p. 11). The same kind of emphasis is found later in the book; Jefferson, Pound says, "was agrarian IN the colonies, and in the U.S.A. of HIS TIME, that is to say a time when, and a place where, there was abundance and superabundance of land" (*JM*, p. 62). Does Pound, or does he not, propose to limit his analysis to the problems of a particular time and place? It is impossible to say. All the capitals and italics in the world cannot pull him out of this quagmire. He surrenders his adherence to the idea of individual civilization that embodies certain permanent human values. Like almost anyone who gets into political discussion, he temporizes.

Jefferson and/or Mussolini cannot be called a fascist book. That label has almost no meaning today, and even if it did mean something, a book so confused defies description by any terms. Today it seems that Pound's fundamental compassion for others and regard for cultural values make it impossible to consider him an adherent of fascism in either a practical or a doctrinaire form.[7] The fact remains, however, that the author of *Jefferson and/or Mussolini* is the victim of the powers of expediency and "opportunism" in the bad and silly sense. Individual civilization is an unhappy institution, especially to an American blessed, or cursed, with an indomitable belief in the efficacy of activist struggle. Pound seems on the whole to be an extreme liberal because of his faith in human improvement; but for a few years at least, he scrapped his ideals for the sake of superficial social order achieved by totalitarian means. He is no better than any other partisan journalist; the fact that he may have been sincere and courageous enough about his convictions to commit himself in public cannot excuse the shabbiness of his expression of his ideas.

Here and there throughout *Jefferson and/or Mussolini* Pound mentions the German anthropologist Leo Frobenius, whose research and theories concern the "organic wholeness" of specific cultures. In a passage titled "Frobenius" Pound says:

The intelligent Teuton said a few bright words, in a recent interview, about the difficulty of communication between civilized men of different races.

"It is not what you tell a man but the part of it that he thinks important that determines the ratio of what is 'communicated' to what is misunderstood."

[*JM*, pp. 32–33]

A few pages later Pound adds, "Frobenius, in the interview referred to, said that Mussolini's miracle had been that of reawakening the sense of responsibility. I cite Frobenius merely to have my own opinion independently delivered by another man who knows enough of the facts to form an intelligent judgment" (*JM*, p. 39). Frobenius comes up again in a chapter called "Paideuma," where Pound says, "I know of no more unpleasant figure in history than the late Franz Josef. Usually a public detestable has some private offset. But of this nullity there is not even record of private pleasantness. And if there's anything in Frobenius' mode of thinking, a people who could tolerate such an emperor and an emperor who could put up with such furniture were well ready for the ash-can" (*JM*, p. 106). The meaning of Frobenius's term *paideuma*—not explained at all in *Jefferson and/or Mussolini*—is not made clear until the "Date Line" of *Make It New* (1934), and even there the tone is still conditional: "However much you accept of Frobenius' theory of *paideuma* as general and overreaching, overstretching the single man, whether you take this as literal fact, or as convenient modus of correlation, the spoken idiom is not only a prime factor, but certainly one of the most potent, progressively so as any modality of civilization ages."[8] Frobenius's thought becomes so important for Pound thereafter that, before looking at *Guide to Kulchur*, I should attempt to describe Frobenius's approach to the "morphology" of organic cultures.

At the same time that Pound was writing in *The Spirit of Romance* that "all ages are contemporaneous," archeologists made a revolutionary discovery along the same lines, as summarized recently by Glyn Daniel:

In 1909 at the Grotte de Valle, near Gibaja (Santander) in north Spain, the Abbé Breuil and Professor Obermaier discovered a classic deposit of one "epoch," namely the Azilian, together with microlithic flints typical of another "epoch," the Tardenoisian. After this, archeologists who had been arguing whether the Azilian came before or after the Tardenoisian could stop arguing. "After this discovery," said Hugo Obermaier, "it could no longer be questioned that the Azilian and the Tardenoisian were contemporary." But what did it mean if two epochs were going to be contemporary? It meant of course that they were not epochs, that the archeologists, who, after all, had developed out of being geologists and had for long been thinking in geological terms of time and fossil-directors, had to rethink their basic principles and think in terms of historical time and man.

All this was really the great moment when prehistoric archeology broke away from the quite understandably inherited conceptions of geology and the natural sciences. The human geographers and anthropologists had for some while been canvassing a new idea with regard to human groupings, and an idea which was to supersede the political idea of nations and tribes.

Ratzel in Germany in the eighties of the nineteenth century had been distinguishing what he called "cultural complexes," and his pupil Leo Frobenius developed this idea and studied what he called "culture-circles."[9]

"Culture" for Pound has two general senses that are combined in his coinage *kulchur*, which suggests both the German *Kultur* and the American commercial-comic practice of altering conventional spellings (e.g., Krazy Kat and Keystone Kops). "Culture" in the sense of superficially refined tastes and manners easily slides into what E. E. Cummings, in a burlesque of an affected accent, calls "keltyer."[10] The younger Pound used the word with a mixture of stylistic caution and social optimism: "The enthusiasm is indiscriminate, but no one can doubt of its presence. The profits of monopoly after monopoly have been poured into the endowments of universities and libraries, and into the collection of works of art. And any hoax that is even labelled 'culture' will sell like patent medicine. . . . I think there has been hardly a scheme proposed for the advancement of 'culture' that has not been accepted and carried out."[11]

Kultur has suffered the same kind of fluctuation of meaning in two languages. Its original usage in German connoted learning and literary culture, but according to one dictionary, the Nazis "perverted it in two directions: (1) 'folklore,' 'race culture'; (2) 'decadent intellectualism,' 'western democratic materialism.'"[12] The *Oxford English Dictionary* sounds uncharacteristically waspish when it says that *Kultur* is "civilization as conceived by the Germans; esp. in a derogatory sense, as involving race-arrogance, militarism, and imperialism." It cites an example from *The Times* for 30 March 1915: "*Kultur*, in fact, has become the exact opposite of 'culture.'"[13] When Pound was requesting money for Joyce from the Royal Literary Fund—also in 1915—he wrote to its secretary, "I assure you that England's thoughtfulness, in the midst of war, in stopping to pension De la Mare, has had a good effect on my country. America will have given England more credit for that small act than she will have given to Germany for a propaganda of Kultur."[14] In 1916 he began a letter to a young disciple with what seems to be a parody of a college catalogue: "KOMPLEAT KULTURE: schedule at 11 227 b 5 q/12/4685."[15] And in 1918 he said, "Kultur is an abomination; philology is an abomination, all repressive uniforming education is an evil."[16] These examples should make clear Pound's reasons for avoiding both "culture" and "Kultur" in the title of his *Guide*, and they may also explain his reluctance to accept Frobenius' ideas without reservation. By 1938, however, he embraced the general concept of cultural morphology. (It seems that he was shifting the center of his attention away from economics and politics as such and toward the underlying cultural patterns and philosophical principles.)

Perhaps the best condensation of what Frobenius meant to Pound is in a letter that Yeats wrote to T. Sturge Moore in 1929: "Ezra Pound has just been in. He says, 'Spengler is a Wells who has founded himself on scholarship instead of English journalism.' He is sunk in Frobenius, Spengler's German source, and finds him a most interesting person. Frobenius suggested the idea that cultures (including arts and sciences) arise out of races, express those races as if they were fruit and leaves in a pre-ordained order and perish with them."[17] In *Jefferson and/or Mussolini*, as we have seen, Pound suggests that both Franz Josef and the ugly furniture at Schönbrunn were symptoms of a single cultural disease (*JM*, p. 106); by the late 1930s he was willing to state, at least in informal letters, that a culture is permeated by a single distinctive unifying spirit, so that if an intelligent man could examine one part of a culture then he could understand the whole. In 1938 he claims, "I can tell the bank-rate and component of tolerance for usury in any epoch by the quality of *line* in painting. Baroque, etc., era of usury becoming tolerated." And in the next year he writes, "I loathe and always have loathed Indian art. Loathed it long before I got my usury axis. Obnubilated, short curves, muddle, jungle, etc. Waaal, we find the hin-goddam-do is a bloody and voracious usurer" (*Ltrs*, pp. 303, 330).

Pound's connection of fashions in art and interest rates is his version of cultural morphology. This development in his thought represents the coalescence of several impulses that are present in his earlier work but are never explicitly joined until the late 1930s, when his struggle toward a coherent view of the political history of the world, his respect for theories that lead to practical discoveries, and his faith in the power of positive action to solve human problems all come together as his *Guide to Kulchur*. More often than not, the interaction between economics and art is expressed by Pound in terms of painting. As early as 1915 he approved a Chinese saying: "As a man's language is an unerring index to his nature, so the actual strokes of his brush in writing or painting betray him and announce either the freedom and nobility of his soul or its meanness and limitation."[18] And as late as 1940 he is passing along to Santayana the "Chinese saying 'a man's character apparent in every one of his brush strokes'" (*Ltrs*, p. 333). According to Pound's morphological synthesis, then, art is doubly reflective: a single stroke of the brush reflects both the character of an artist and the spirit of his culture.

Frobenius says in *Paideuma* that his career in anthropology began the moment he realized, at the age of twenty-one, that "die menschliche Kultur ein selbständiges organisches Wesen sei."[19] This idea permits the reduction of cultural complexities to sets of related phenomena explained by reference to *Altersklassen*, much as one might explain someone's behavior by saying that he is only acting his age. Frobenius' analogy of the cultural "organism" is worked out in great detail, and the spirit of the analogy, the principle of growth in a culture, is given the name *paideuma*. In Greek *paideuma* means "the taught" in both the senses that the term can have in English: the person who is taught and the material that is taught to him. Frobenius uses this word in order to avoid certain prejudices that might inhere in *Kultur*—a motive that Pound would certainly understand.[20]

Frobenius provides a tabular display of the *Grundlagen des Paideuma* in which the stages of growth in a culture are aligned with the childhood, youth, and maturity of an individual. For each stage of the growth of a culture, for example, there are characteristic *Raumlichkeiten* and *Zeitlichkeiten*—senses of space and time. The sense of space in the childhood of culture is confined to the community: it expands in the youth of a culture to embrace a whole people (*Volk*); and in the maturity of a culture the sense of space comprehends "regions of the ecumene." The sense of time, correspondingly, proceeds through stages of growth called "un-historical," "historical," and "superhistorical" (*ungeschichtlicht, geschichtlich*, and *übergeschichtlich*).[21]

Such schemes suggest the futility of Edward Casaubon's grandiose project in *Middlemarch*. Mr. Casaubon is there engaged in an undertaking that will show "that all the mythical systems or erratic mythical fragments in the world were corruptions of a tradition originally revealed. Having once mastered the true position and taken a firm footing there, the vast field of mythical constructions became intelligible, nay, luminous with the reflected light of correspondences."[22] As guidance for practical anthropological work, Frobenius' idea of organic growth is not just a visionary dream but a positive danger, because it can easily prejudice a researcher. In *Philosophy in a New Key*, Susanne K. Langer cites Frobenius as an example of the early ethnologists who were "mystified by the high seriousness of actions that looked purely clownish and farcical to the European beholder; just as the Christian missionaries had long reported the difficulty of making the gospels plausible to men who were able to believe stories far more mysterious and fantastic in their own idiom." She describes Frobenius' early attitudes:

Frobenius . . . describes an initiation ceremony in New South Wales, in the course of which the older men performed a dog-dance, on all fours, for the benefit of the young acolytes who watched these rites, preliminary to the painful honor of having a tooth knocked out. Frobenius refers to the ritual as a "comedy," a "farce," and is amazed at the solemnity with which the boys sat through the "ridiculous canine display." "They acted as if they never caught sight of the comical procession of men." A little later he describes a funeral among the Bougala, in the Southern Congo; again, each step in the performance seems to him a circus act. . . . The professor is at a loss to understand how even the least intelligent of men can reach such depths of folly.[23]

Guy Davenport, in a largely unsuccessful attempt to defend Frobenius from Mrs. Langer, says that "the former account of the ritual dog-dance is accurately described, the emotional words 'farce' and 'ridiculous canine display' not eliciting ridicule of the

Bengal aborigines' initiation rite but conveying almost soberly the antic preliminary of what Frobenius describes sympathetically as a solemn ceremony."[24] I do not know why Davenport moves the ceremony from New South Wales to Bengal, nor do I know how the words "ridiculous canine display" can elicit anything but ridicule. Trying to redeem Frobenius from "chronic disregard and misrepresentation," Davenport says of Mrs. Langer's remarks: "Criticism which neglects twenty-eight years of a man's work, choosing to consider a first book rather than forty-odd later ones, has made of Frobenius also a genuine 'man of no fortune and with a name to come.' "[25] But Mrs. Langer is not criticizing Frobenius' whole career; she is legitimately using an early work of his as a good example of the response of early ethnologists to alien customs.

Unlike Davenport, I believe that Frobenius' work has been sufficiently recognized for what it is: the contribution of one pioneer among many. There is no conspiracy to obscure his achievement. It is simply a fact that his researches have been superseded by studies that are more comprehensive and objective. Critical interest in Frobenius today is based largely on his importance to Pound's thought.[26]

There is evidence that Pound considered borrowing Frobenius' title *Paideuma* for the book he began in 1937—"wot Ez knows, all of it, fer 7 an sax pence"; subsequently he rejected *The New Learning* and *Guide to Kultur* and settled on *Guide to Kulchur*.[27] Far removed from the scatterbrained *Jefferson and/or Mussolini*, *Guide to Kulchur*, the entertaining synthesis of thirty years of work on the problem of civilization, is also one of Pound's most readable books.

In addition to the term *paideuma* itself, Frobenius contributed material to fill out Pound's conception of one coherent world. With works by Frobenius or his disciples at hand, Pound could add items from African and Australian lore to a domain that already included matter from Europe, Asia, and the Americas. It seems, however, that Pound uses cultural morphology more as a general attitude toward history than as a means for studying any particular manifestations of a given culture. The idea of the *paideuma* may not work as a particularly useful or powerful tool for research in the social sciences, but for Pound it serves the purpose of integrating the body of his social thought.

Guide to Kulchur is, of course, less a *summa* than a long informal essay—it is Pound's *Biographia Literaria*.[28] It should not, however, be dismissed as nothing more than the chaotic discharge of an unstable mind. Donald Davie has ridiculed the book just as though it were indistinguishable from *Jefferson and/or Mussolini*. He finds no coherent structure in *Guide to Kulchur*, but at the same time he manages to locate enough uniformity in its opinions to make a very serious charge: "*Guide to Kulchur* is an overtly Fascist book." Davie opens his charge with a citation of Pound's incidental use of "totalitarian" and then presents further evidence:

Pound even compliments Wyndham Lewis on having discovered Hitler before he, Pound, discovered Mussolini. Though one dislikes admitting it, nothing has happened since to invalidate this logical and chronological connection between modernism in the arts and Fascism in politics; Thomas Mann discerned it also. There is further corroboration in Chapter 21, where the Vou club in totalitarian Japan, with which Pound corresponds through Katue Kitasono, is said to have been founded by admirers of Satie.

In some places Pound's Fascism is just a straightforward enthusiasm for all things Italian, no more sophisticated (despite his years of residence in Rapallo) than the enthusiasm of any British or American middle-aged couple after a holiday in Sestri Levante.[29]

Pound does acknowledge Lewis's "discovery" of Hitler as a "superior perception,"[30] but there is no other reference to Hitler in the book. The fact that Pound is a modernist, however, no more confirms his fascism than does his correspondence with a Japanese poet. The cases of Pablo Neruda and Hugh MacDiarmid, distinguished modernist poets who both ran for political office as communists, ought to do something to invalidate the connection between modernism and fascism. And it is clear in *Guide to Kulchur*, as in *Jefferson and/or Mussolini*, that Pound has nothing at all like an "enthusiasm for all things Italian"; even if he did feel such enthusiasm, that fact would lend no corroboration whatever to a charge of fascism. *Guide to Kulchur* deserves much closer scrutiny than Davie has given to it.

To discover the *paideuma*—the vital spirit of a given civilization, the cultural total of its achievements—of a society, Frobenius would proceed deductively. Believing beforehand that the society must be in a certain stage of development, he would look for patterns of thought and perception that accompany the childhood, youth, or maturity of any culture. The method of *Guide to Kulchur*, on the other hand, is largely inductive. Pound arranges cultural particulars in such juxtapositions that the reader can usually see for himself that there is indeed some kind of connection. The "ideogram," working like a collage of elements that are disparate but interdependent, is Pound's primary instrument for both discovering and delineating the *paideuma*.

In one place Pound calls his own work "a book of yatter" (*GK*, p. 292), but he suggests an interesting justification for his seemingly immethodical improvisations. The frontispiece is a picture of a wafer of wax bearing the profile of Salustio Malatesta. In an accompanying note Pound discusses the level of the Malatesta family's civilization in terms that could easily apply also to himself and his own book: "If you consider the Malatesta and Sigismundo in particular, a failure, he was at all events a failure worth all the successes of his age. He had in Rimini, Pisanello, Pier della Francesca. Rimini still has 'the best Bellini in Italy.' If the Tempio is a jumble and junk shop, it nevertheless registers a concept. There is no other single man's effort equally registered" (*GK*, p. 2). In the middle of the book, he contrasts Sigismundo Malatesta's individual spirit with the zeitgeist of fifteenth-century Italy: "The Tempio Malatestiano is both an apex and in verbal sense a monumental failure. It is perhaps the apex of what one man has embodied in the last 1000 years of the occident. *I.* cultural 'high' is marked. . . . All that a single man could, Malatesta managed *against* the current of power. You can contrast it with St. Hilaire. You can contrast it with ANY great summit done WITH the current of power" (*GK*, pp. 159–60). An artist in harmony with his time may produce coherent and orderly works; a man out of key may produce only a "jumble"—like the Tempio or *Guide to Kulchur*—but the jumble can superlatively register the energy of one individual's civilization.

But that kind of triumph is clearly unsatisfactory. The Pound of *Guide to Kulchur* is not content with his individual civilization; he would clearly prefer to move with the current of power for the sake of his art. Having lived for thirty years in voluntary exile, he is no longer able to fall back on his parochial status as an American. He therefore embraces a concept of ecumenical culture that is shared by all "citizens of the world"; to give a name to this new civilization he borrows the term *paideuma*:

> The Paideuma is not the Zeitgeist, though I have no doubt many people will try to sink it in the latter romantic term. Napoleon said he failed for opposing the spirit of his time.[31]
> As I understand it, Frobenius has seized a word not current for the express purpose of scraping off the barnacles and "atmosphere" of a long-used term.
> When I said I wanted a new civilization, I think I cd. have used Frobenius' term.
> At any rate for my own use and for the duration of this treatise I shall use Paideuma for the gristly roots of ideas that are in action.
> I shall leave "Zeitgeist" as including also the atmospheres, the tints of mental air and the idées reçues, the notions that a great mass of people still hold or half hold from habit, from waning custom.
>
> [*GK*, pp. 57–58]

From his global point of view, he writes his *Guide to Kulchur* that is essentially a new *Patria Mia*, but the *patria* is neither the United States nor the informal republic of homeless men of letters. The new *patria* is the *paideuma* of human civilization that can be manifest in all places at all times. Pound's use of *paideuma* is rather far removed from Frobenius', but he is pursuing Frobenius' idea of a mature culture that thinks in ecumenical terms from a "super-historical" point of view.

With his new control over his perceptions of culture—so unlike the befuddlement and hysteria of *Jefferson and/or Mussolini*—Pound is buoyantly witty, mixing personal reminiscence with detailed commentary on such other guides to culture as the *Analects* of

Confucius and the *Nicomachean Ethics*. His range seems practically
unlimited. Although he jumps easily from subject to subject, the
book does not give the sense of chaos. Pound's purpose is to present
examples of culture—in costume, cuisine, and etiquette as well as
in the arts and sciences:

> Men of my time have witnessed "parties" in London gardens where, as I
> recall it, everyone else (male) wore grey "toppers." As I remember it even
> Henry James wore one, and unless memory blends two occasions he wore
> also an enormous checked weskit. Men have witnessed the dinner cere-
> mony on flagships, where the steward still called it "claret" and a bath
> oliver appeared with the cheese. (Stilton? I suppose it must have been
> stilton.)
>
> Such activities may be called natural phenomena, to be distinguished
> from more numerous "efforts," by which I mean social events whereunder
> one sensed a heave, an habitual outlay.
>
> I isolate social habit, custom indicating high culture, from exceptional
> individuals, let us say those who have made history or at least appeared in
> the story.
>
> Apart from things seen, and more pertinent to my ideogram at this
> moment: von X. who had never been out of uniform from the time he was
> six until the end of the "war" (1919).
>
> *I am not in these slight memories, merely "pickin' daisies." A man does not
> know his own* ADDRESS *(in time) until he knows where his time and milieu
> stand in relation to other times and conditions.*
>
> Countess M. (an italian title) counted her high water mark a wedding at
> the court in St. Petersburg.
>
> [*GK*, pp. 82–83]

Pound is showing the reader what and how a civilized man thinks
about life as a whole, so that he is willing to make connections
between elements heretofore unrelated, as when he calls Gorgias
(fifth century B.C.) a dadaist (*GK*, p. 120). And again, as in *Patria
Mia* and his first letters to Harriet Monroe twenty-five years earlier,
he foresees a renaissance: "Plenty of chance for a NEW Quattro-
cento" (*GK*, p. 344).

Guide to Kulchur, now forty years in the past, is the last complete statement in prose of Pound's social thought. The book called
Impact: Essays on Ignorance and the Decline of American Civilization
that appeared in 1960 consists mostly of condensed and expurgated

versions of scattered pieces of journalism that Pound turned out between 1927 and 1944. Noel Stock, the editor, is in effect as much the author of *Impact* as Pound is, for almost nothing appears in its original form. The book is to be handled, therefore, with a good deal of circumspection. As it turns out, there is very little in it that adds to what we already know about Pound's later social thought from reading *Jefferson and/or Mussolini* and *Guide to Kulchur*.

Frobenius' name is mentioned frequently in the pieces in *Impact*. It is evident that as late as 1937 Pound was committed heavily to the concept of racial determinism: "Communism is Muscovite, Socialism is German and embodies the worst defect of that race, democracy with representation divided in respect to geographical areas is Anglo-American, and the corporate state is latin."[32] In "The Jefferson-Adams Letters as a Shrine and a Monument" (1937), he speaks as an American:

> If we are a nation, we must have a national mind. Frobenius escaped both the fiddling term "culture" and rigid "Kultur" by recourse to greek, he used "Paideuma" with a meaning that is necessary to almost all serious discussion of such subjects as that are now under discussion. His "Paideuma" means the mental formation, the inherited habits of thought, the conditionings, aptitudes of a given race or time.
>
> In Italy there is current the adjective "antistorico" to describe unlikely proposals; ideologies hung in a vacuum or contrary to the natural order of events as conditioned by race, time and geography.
>
> [*Impact*, p. 168]

Not until *Guide to Kulchur* does Pound consolidate the enlarged meaning of *paideuma* as the spirit of a new civilization of world culture. During the Second World War, as some of the pieces in *Impact* clearly demonstrate, he reverts to the hysteria of *Jefferson and/or Mussolini*; and this is a reversion that no amount of editorial legerdemain can conceal.

In "A Visiting Card" (1942) Pound makes a case for Brooks Adams as a kind of American Frobenius: "This member of the Adams family, son of C. F. Adams, grandson of J. Q. Adams, and great-grandson of J. Adams, Father of the Nation, was, as far as I know, the first to formulate the idea of *Kulturmorphologie* in

America."[33] Along with such items as Confucius, Homer, Dante, and American Constitution, and Frobenius, the list of books labelled "As Sextant" in the "Addenda: 1952" section of *Guide to Kulchur* includes the following: "BROOKS ADAMS: Law of Civilization and Decay: most recent summary of 'where in a manner of speaking' we had got to half a century ago" (*GK*, p. 352). A relatively neglected member of the Adams dynasty, he practices cultural morphology with a "usury axis" and a racial emphasis that both appealed to Pound:

> The theory proposed is based upon the accepted scientific principle that the law of force and energy is of universal application in nature, and that animal life is one of the outlets through which solar energy is dissipated.
> Starting from this fundamental proposition, the first deduction is, that, as human societies are forms of animal life, these societies must differ among themselves in energy, in proportion as nature has endowed them, more or less abundantly with energetic material.[34]

Depending on a racist concept of national character that now sounds very shabby indeed, Adams uses pseudoscientific means to trace the history of the exploitation and waste of resources from Rome down to modern times. "Roman civilization," he says, "was less complex than modern because of the relative inflexibility of the Latin mind." A little later he comments that an allowance of a dollar per month in silver is "too little to sustain any but the most tenacious organisms, even among Asiatics."[35] I am not plucking these remarks from their context—their whole context is little more than a tissue of such observations that support racism with scientific jargon. In the culmination of one argument, Adams says, "As velocity augments and competition intensifies, nature begins to sift the economic minds themselves, culling a favoured aristocracy of the craftiest and subtlest types; choosing, for example, the Armenian in Byzantium, the Marwari in India, and the Jew in London."[36] This is a long way from Homer and Dante, and it ought to be below the notice of the usually generous and perspicacious world citizen who wrote a *Guide to Kulchur* in 1937 that is still useful today.

The general course of Pound's social thought follows lines that can be summarized in temporal and spatial terms. In *The Spirit of Romance*, *Patria Mia*, and other early works he speaks as an American-born world citizen who sees in Walt Whitman the embodiment of the spirit of a particular time and place. Whitman as avatar is contrasted with Dante and Villon, who wrote, respectively, above and below the zeitgeist of their surroundings. Later Pound denigrates the vulgarity of Whitman, toward whom he is always ambivalent, as indeed he is toward America as a whole. He honors Henry James as America's antiself who built with his works a countervailing "continent" that preserves the American scene and idiom without sharing America's vices and follies. Around 1920 this idea of the antiself as the best expression of a national civilization is superseded by the Gourmontian idea of supranational individual civilization shared by the members of the informal republic of the *Heimatlos*. (Significantly, Pound can find no English word that registers the idea of *patria* or *Heimat*.) From this low point of isolation and despair, Pound rises to an attitude of optimism based on the unifying concept of the *paideuma*, which is first emphasized as the keynote of a particular race at a particular time. Mussolini, far from being antistorico, is perfectly in tune with the *paideuma* of modern Italy, as Jefferson was with the *paideuma* of the early years of the United States. The idea of the *paideuma* is then enlarged in *Guide to Kulchur* to comprehend world civilization that transcends time and space. This second phase of Pound's hopeful search for a new renaissance of civilization collapses during the Second World War; thereafter his fatigue and dismay are reflected in the fact that no more whole books devoted to social thought appear.

POUND'S POETICS
3 OF TIME AND TIMELESSNESS

Ezra Pound's ideas about space and time are realized in subordinate ideas about culture; his ideas about culture are, in turn, realized in practical criticism of political and poetic structures; and finally, his practical literary criticism is actively carried over into poems. However shaky his political thinking, there is nothing uncertain about his critical ideas, although a degree of subtlety is necessary for the reader to separate Pound's critical maxims from what actually takes place in his poems.

Pound's poetics cannot be found in a single volume. The principal outlines can be discerned in *A B C of Reading*, but that book is little more than a dilation of the long essay "How to Read." Details and examples can be found in miscellaneous essays and reviews, most of which were written between 1910 and 1931. Here I shall examine Pound's major critical work to see how it handles the historical and cultural concepts outlined above in Chapters 1 and 2.

When writing about novels or plays, Pound often dwells on issues of biography, audience, and working conditions; when dealing with poetry, however, he becomes emphatically formal and technical, and it is in the detailed criticism of poetry that his aesthetic writing has been most abundant and most durable. *A B C of Reading* and "How to Read" could be called *A B C of Reading Poetry* and "How to Read Poetry." For these reasons, the essence of Pound's criticism of novels—since it deals mainly with problems of social thought—has already been discussed above, especially in the passages that concern Henry James and James Joyce.

Pound's criticism, which remained much more consistent than his cultural and political thought, treats two major aspects of poetry: mimesis and expression. Poetry imitates certain objects (actions, characters, states of mind) by means of the power of words to cast images, make music, and appeal to the imagination. By the quality of imitation, furthermore, a poem is "polysemous," to use Dante's term; a poem can imitate several objects at once because the objects themselves bear mimetic and analogical linkages one to another. Words, let us say, represent an action (for example, a journey); and this action, in turn, represents a more general action (for example, the course of a life). By further extensions, the "curriculum" of one man's life can represent the course of all human life; and that course, subsumed under a general metaphor of organic change, can represent the fate of all things under the aspects of time and eternity. Taken as a whole, the concentric aesthetic act of polysemous mimesis suggests a second universe of representation as well, because the work of art, in addition to imitating objects, expresses the individual maker at a particular time, his total character up to the time of the making, the specific character of his circumstances (zeitgeist or *paideuma*), and again, as *this* circle widens, the whole human condition.

Pound's aesthetic of mimesis and expression was crystallized around a set of terms—luminous detail, image, persona, vortex, ideogram—that all suggest an objective correlative that the poet uses to externalize certain internal states. The poet ought to articulate his own set of correlatives in such a way that the reader can experience similar states of mind. To this extent Pound's aesthetic is merely technical. It takes on a moral dimension, however, as soon as it is recognized that the medium of poetic imitation is also the medium of social communication and that a language thrives or suffers in proportion to the nourishment or abuse it receives in the work of its poets. The relation between the imitating work and the particular zeitgeist that it expresses is another factor in the moral dimension of the work of art—a factor that embodies the social and political values of a culture. If the character of the artist is in harmony with the character of his surroundings and if these respective characters are virtuous, the works of art will receive support from their cultures. On the other hand, if the artist's character is radically out of key with his surroundings, the work may still be the culmination of one man's individual civilization, like Sigismundo Malatesta's Tempio in Rimini, but, fragmentary and incomplete, it will lack logical consistency and aesthetic integrity.

Such, in outline, is my conception of Pound's aesthetics. Space and time are obviously important considerations in this kind of thinking, because the aesthetic act is concentrated precisely on transcending its own physical limits and on removing the object and the audience from their conditions of spatiality and temporality by putting them into a refreshing and illuminating connection with free, timeless values.

But how? Poetry exists in time and therefore best imitates objects that are arranged sequentially. For objects that are arranged in a timeless pattern of simultaneous relations, the spatial media provide the best expression. In Pound's aesthetic there is a search for means by which the immediate impact of spatial arts can be achieved by words in time. Pound accepts the assumption that time and space are properties of the real world and its aesthetic counterpart, but he rejects the conclusion that poetry is limited by its own temporality to the imitation of temporal objects; he seeks a form of art that combines all the virtues of painting and poetry.

In criticism as in social thought, Pound is seldom systematic or thorough. He first gathered his scattered technical observations, some dating back to 1911, in an essay called "A Retrospect" that appeared in his *Pavannes and Divisions* (1918). Here he justifies his immethodical approach: "Criticism is not a circumscription or a set of prohibitions. It provides fixed points of departure. It may startle a dull reader into alertness. That little of it which is good is mostly in stray phrases; or if it be an older artist helping a younger it is in great measure but rules of thumb, cautions gained by experience."[1] (A few years later T. S. Eliot said that there is no critical method "except to be very intelligent."[2]) In "A Retrospect" Pound reproduces the imagist principles supposedly agreed on in 1912 by Hilda Doolittle, Richard Aldington, and himself. Even construed as temporary rules of thumb, these three laws governing treatment, vocabulary, and rhythm are so vaguely stated that their terms can be adjusted to praise or condemn almost any work of art. The first principle—"Direct treatment of the 'thing' whether subjective or objective" (*LE*, p. 3)—contains only one term ("direct") to which any definite meaning can be attached; and immediately one can imagine any number of circumstances in which the poet may properly be allowed the indirect treatment of a thing, especially a subjective thing. Similar reservations apply to the second principle—"To use absolutely no word that does not contribute to the presentation" (*LE*, p. 3). It is easy to feel that a word in a certain poem is inert—possessing nothing but metrical value, if indeed any value at all; but again one can imagine any number of instances in which the "presentation" of an objective or subjective thing requires the use of lexical or syntactic devices that under different circumstances might seem quite worthless. Dramatic verse is full of "bad" poetry that is perfectly suited to its purpose because its very obscurity, clumsiness, or inertness serves to reveal a character. The third imagist principle—"As regarding rhythm: to compose in the sequence of the musical phrase, not in the sequence of the metronome" (*LE*, p. 3)—is the least objectionable because its proscription of monotonous rhythms, even though *they* may occasionally be appropriate, accords with most readers' feelings about sing-song verse. As appealing as the negative half of this third principle may be, its positive endorsement of the "musical phrase" as the unit of poetic sequence is as vague as the arguments of the first two principles. A musical phrase is infinitely variable: within the limits of one "measure" of a given time signature, an endless series of endlessly subdivided units of both sound and silence is possible. Such unlimited variety is probably more attractive than monotony, but since the "musical phrase" is so variable, not much value can be derived from the use of its sequence—its sequence can be anything. This kind of license is as monotonous as monotony.

The celebrated imagist principles are too weak to have much value either as practical advice or as aesthetic doctrine. What remains interesting about them today is their opposition to limitations of time. They are against the "time," in the historical sense, that imposes conventions of excessive obliquity and elaboration on the treatment of the subject of poetry; they are against the "time," in what can be called the "chronometronomic" sense, that imposes mechanical patterns on the musically flexible contours of poetry.

Time is also an important factor in "A Few Don'ts" (originally in *Poetry* for March 1913), another of the emphatic documents collected in "A Retrospect." Here Pound defines an image as "that which presents an intellectual and emotional complex in an instant of time." He describes this presentation, not in terms of its structure, but in terms of its effect on the reader: "It is the presentation of such a 'complex' instantaneously which gives that sense of sudden liberation; that sense of freedom from time limits and space limits; that sense of sudden growth, which we experience in the presence of the greatest works of art" (*LE*, p. 4). Here, with such complex notions as "instant of time" and "sudden growth," Pound is far beyond the kind of technical rules of thumb that one would pass along to apprentices.

Since the means for achieving these effects of sudden liberation and growth still need to be clarified, it may help to look at one of Pound's imagist poems and his comments on it. In April 1913, one month after the appearance of his "A Few Don'ts," *Poetry* printed "In a Station of the Metro":

> *The apparition of these faces in the crowd;*
> *Petals on a wet, black bough.* [3]

The poem clearly demonstrates the imagist principles of economy and variable phrasing; the problem of the directness of treatment is handled by Pound in an article called "How I Began" that was published soon after the poem appeared:

For well over a year I have been trying to make a poem of a very beautiful thing that befell me in the Paris Underground. I got out of a train at, I think, La Concorde and in the jostle I saw a beautiful face, and then, turning suddenly, another and another, and then a beautiful child's face, and then another beautiful face. All that day I tried to find words for what this made me feel. That night as I went home along the rue Raynouard I was still trying. I could get nothing but spots of colour. I remember thinking that if I had been a painter I might have started a wholly new school of painting. I tried to write the poem weeks afterwards in Italy, but found it useless. Then only the other night, wondering how I should tell the adventure, it struck me that in Japan, where a work of art is not estimated by its acreage and where sixteen syllables are counted enough for a poem if you arrange and punctuate them properly, one might make a very little poem which would be translated about as follows:—

"*The apparition of these faces in the crowd:*
"*Petals on a wet, black bough.*"

And there, or in some other very old, very quiet civilisation, some one else might understand the significance.[4]

The same anecdote is elaborated in "Vorticism," an essay that was printed in the *Fortnightly Review* for 1 September 1914 and was later included in *Gaudier-Brzeska* (1916). Here Pound describes his tactic for escaping the sequential presentation inherent in the verbal medium, and he uses many of the same terms—notably "sudden" and "instant"—that occur in his earlier definition of *image*:

The "one image poem" is a form of super-position, that is to say, it is one idea set on top of another. I found it useful in getting out of the impasse in which I had been left by my metro emotion. I wrote a thirty-line poem, and destroyed it because it was what we call a work "of second intensity." Six months later I made a poem half that length; a year later I made the following hokku-like sentence:—

The apparition of these faces in the crowd:
Petals on a wet, black bough.

I dare say it is meaningless unless one has drifted into a certain vein of thought. In a poem of this sort one is trying to record the precise instant when a thing outward and objective transforms itself, or darts into a thing inward and subjective.[5]

Pound's definition of *image*, as displayed in the two-line poem and his comments on its development, is an early step in his journey to discover aesthetic devices that make it possible for the ostensibly time-bound verbal medium to escape time and to express, instantaneously, moments or complexes of sudden illumination.

In "Vorticism" Pound cites a Japanese poem that is so concentrated it seems to need parenthetical enlargement to make its meaning clear:

Victor Plarr tells me that once, when he was walking over snow with a Japanese naval officer, they came to a place where a cat had crossed the path, and the officer said, "Stop, I am making a poem." Which poem was, roughly, as follows:—

> "The footsteps of the cat upon the snow:
> (are like) plum-blossoms."

The words "are like" would not occur in the original, but I add them for clarity.[6]

Pound is repeating a gesture that he employed in *The Spirit of Romance*. There, explanatory phrases are inserted in translations of difficult lines. Pound says in a footnote, "I have thought it necessary to insert in brackets the subjects of some of the relative pronouns."[7] Such explanations are usually not necessary and may even seem intrusive, but Pound apparently feels constrained to make the meaning of other people's poetry as clear as possible. At any rate, in his own "hokku-like" poem that is similar to the Japanese officer's, there is no explicit verbal indication of likeness between the two juxtaposed—or superposed—images. Indeed, there is no verb at all.

The Japanese officer's poem, which seems rather trifling, capitalizes on the simple fact that paw prints and blossoms look alike. As in Housman's lyric about the cherry trees hung with snow, the harmony between the visual patterns of footprints (seen) and petals (recalled) accents the irony in the fact that a winter scene can suggest an image of spring. To be sure, this procedure is one way of collapsing temporal and discursive sequences by means of a compressed comparison, but it hardly seems to be powerful or versatile enough to sustain a whole aesthetic doctrine. Fortunately, Pound's Metro poem, although it too uses an image of petals and suppresses the verbal expression of the simile, seems quite a bit more complex than the footprint-blossom poem. Pound's poem enjoys the additional quality of mystery. Instead of a pat equation of visual images already laden with accepted meanings, it offers two parallel patterns of mysterious vision. (Without his testimony in "How I Began" and "Vorticism," we would have no way of being sure that he thought the faces in the station were uniformly beautiful, nor would we know how intensely the personal experience had affected him.) Two senses of "apparition"—both "appearance" in the simplest sense as well as "spirit"—seem to be at work in the poem; using a word with two meanings at once is another device for avoiding temporal sequence. The faces are seen in a way that suggests disembodiment, and their apparitional quality, whether beautiful or not, is emphasized by the setting of an underground station that, even sixty years ago and even with art nouveau metal flowers for entrance decoration, must have been dismal. The mysterious vision by which Pound was so challenged and disturbed generates an antithetical vision, a pastoral image of petals, but it too is mysterious. The flesh-colored, face-shaped petals seem to have fallen during a spring shower and come to rest on a lower branch. The rapid succession of the image of faces and the "afterimage" of petals produces a composite image—"spots of colour"—that gives virtually instantaneous expression to an emotional and intellectual complex. It is not possible to paraphrase this complex faithfully in any words other than those of the poem, but its components, very crudely stated, seem to include love for the life and beauty of the faces and petals along with grief for their attachment to some dark, nearly infernal tubular structure, whether an underground tunnel or a wet, black bough.[8] (A polyglot may be aware that the root of "Metro" means "mother" and also yields the name "Demeter.")

During his imagist-vorticist period Pound became the literary executor of Ernest Fenollosa, who had left a mass of notes on oriental literature when he died in 1908. In this material Pound found confirmation of his belief in concentration and economy. For example, Fenollosa is invoked in one of Pound's letters written to the young poet Iris Barry in 1916:

"Wet Morning": "Too tender to have become grimed" is a weak line. I am sorry about your holidays, also you should have a chance to see Fenollosa's big essay on verbs, mostly on verbs. Heaven knows when I shall get it printed. He inveighs against "IS," wants transitive verbs. "Become" is as weak as "is." Let the grime do something to the leaves. "All nouns come from verbs." To primitive man, a thing only IS what it does. That is Fenollosa, but I think the theory is a very good one for poets to go by.[9]

One can try to imagine Pound's feelings about "Too tender to have become grimed," which has a good deal wrong with it that could never be repaired by simple manipulation of verbs; but he was sympathetic. (Often there is not much to say to a poet who has done poor work, especially if he is a friend whose feelings one does not want to hurt needlessly. In such cases, a modest technical suggestion may be quite in order. Faced with some dog's breakfast of incompetently articulated pomposity and sentimentality, many a critic has said something like, "Maybe it would work better if you put it into the third person instead of the first.")

Habitually ecumenical in his scope, Pound championed Fenollosa's ideas about the inherent superiority of the Chinese written language as a vehicle for poetry. Today Fenollosa's thinking, like Frobenius', is of interest chiefly because it meant something to Pound; "The Chinese Written Character as a Medium for Poetry" —which appeared, heavily edited by Pound, in the *Little Review* in 1919—is deeply flawed by its ignorance and prejudice regarding both linguistics and aesthetics.

One's own language becomes stale with use, and it is refreshing from time to time to become familiar with other ways of saying things and other things to say, the more foreign the better. A friend of mine once lamented, for example, that in English we have only "popcorn," a word expressive enough in its own way but inferior to the Spanish *palomitas de maiz*—"little doves of corn." A lobster is called "dragon-shrimp" in Chinese, and an owl is a "cat-headed eagle." There is a story in which an Englishman, a Frenchman, and an Italian rhapsodize over the merits of *butterfly*, *papillon*, and *farfalla*, whereupon a German pounds on the table and demands to know what is wrong with *Schmetterling*. But the usual attitude toward one's own language is discontent, which applies to syntax as well as vocabulary. There are times when English patterns force a writer to place his emphasis in an awkward manner that could be avoided if his language had the flexibility of Latin or the economy of Chinese. An English writer ordinarily must use explicit pronouns, for example, that would be absorbed into verb inflections in Latin; *ego* occurs much less frequently in Latin than *I* does in English. In Vietnamese and Chinese the usual way of saying "My name is Smith" amounts to "Name I Smith"; I have been told that the use of a verb in such situations, although it is permissible, may sound unduly insistent—"My name *is* Smith." For Fenollosa, an amateur as linguist and critic, the appeal of Chinese grammar was increased by the peculiarities of the Chinese system of writing—which is more or less ideographic, unlike the more or less phonetic European system.

Modern logicians—following the researches of Frege, Russell, and Wittgenstein—have tried to supplement ordinary writing with pictures and mathematical symbols that approach the ideal of *Begriffsschrift*, a way of representing concepts without verbal or grammatical prejudice to their integrity.[10] In his unsophisticated devotion to Chinese, Fenollosa handled the same sort of problem at a much lower level of complexity; but for Pound's purposes Fenollosa's essay was prized as "a study of the fundamentals of all aesthetics."[11] Of Chinese poetry in general, Fenollosa says, "It speaks at once with the vividness of painting, and with the mobility of sounds. It is, in some sense, more objective than either, more dramatic. In reading Chinese we do not seem to be juggling mental counters, but to be watching *things* work out their own fate." (If this be true, either as a fact or as an aesthetic illusion, then no "treatment of the thing" could be more "direct.") He goes on to prescribe techniques for the translation of such active poetry: "We should beware of English grammar, its hard parts of speech, and its lazy satisfaction with nouns and adjectives. We should seek and at least bear in mind the verbal undertone of each noun. We should avoid 'is' and bring in a wealth of neglected English verbs. Most of the existing translations violate all of these rules." And here Pound adds a note: "These precautions should be broadly conceived. It is not so much their letter, as the underlying feeling of objectification and activity, that matters."[12]

Around 1920, when Pound's critical thinking began to attain its final form, he could see some of his ideas dynamically in action in several distinguished periodicals and in the work of Yeats, Eliot, and Williams; so there was less need for him to continue his strenuous campaign against bad art. The listing of his contributions to periodicals in Donald Gallup's bibliography contains about ninety items each for 1919 and 1920; then the figure goes down to twenty-two in 1921, fourteen in 1922, and six in 1923. There are only three items listed for 1926, and none of them have to do with literature—two concern politics and one is about the musician George Antheil.[13] The bulk of his criticism after that time is found in three works, all of which are pedagogical in purpose and design: "How to Read" (1929), *A B C of Reading* (1934), and the anthology *Confucius to Cummings* (1964), edited by Pound and Marcella Spann.

The imagist documents of the period between 1912 and 1920 contain most of Pound's early technical criticism. The central problem there, as we have seen, is discovering the means for subverting the temporal sequence of language so that images can present the essence or effect of sudden illuminations that transcend space and time. "How to Read," written when he was in his early forties, is his first sustained attempt to give his aesthetic of technique a semblance of organization. "Great literature," he says here, "is simply language charged with meaning to the utmost possible degree" (*LE*, p. 23).[14] This maximal charge of meaning presumably makes of a linguistic construct the highly efficient concentration—image, vortex, ideogram—that presents an emotional and intellectual complex so directly and so powerfully that its operation *seems*, at any rate, to take but an instant of time.

This instant of sudden illumination that collapses time and space is invoked in a letter from Pound to his father in 1927, not long before "How to Read." Giving an "outline of main scheme" of *The Cantos*, he lists three chief subjects, among them "the 'magic moment' or moment of metamorphosis, bust thru from quotidien into 'divine or permanent world.'"[15] The power of words to record the moment of transcendence when an objective thing is metamorphosed into either an inward subjective experience or an ideal entity—called respectively the "darting into" and the "bust thru" —is the mysterious force that Pound's criticism works to elucidate.[16]

To explain the charging of language, Pound uses in "How to Read" a set of terms—*melopoeia, phanopoeia,* and *logopoeia*—that first appeared in his writings around 1918.[17] Melopoeia, which covers the musical qualities of poetry, projects "a force tending often to lull, or to distract the reader from the exact sense of the language." Here he makes a claim for melopoeia that relates it to his preoccupation with metamorphosis: "It is poetry on the borders of music and music is perhaps the bridge between consciousness and the unthinking sentient or even insentient universe" (*LE*, p. 26).

Aside from this power to link consciousness with its surroundings, melopoeia is the simplest of the means of charging language, and it is the one that Pound dealt with most in his earlier technical criticism. In "A Few Don'ts" (1913) he suggested that "the candidate fill his mind with the finest cadences he can discover, preferably in a foreign language, so that the meaning of the words may be less likely to divert his attention from the movement" (*LE*, p. 5). According to "How to Read," the three functional categories of melopoeia—speech, chant, and song—cut across the two structural categories, melody and rhythm (*LE*, p. 28). Melody comprises such arrangements of sounds as alliteration, assonance, and rhyme; and since syllables vary in length and stress, rhythmic patterns can be built up of various clusters of "feet" arranged by meter or by number of syllables.

As early as the introduction to his first translations of the poems of Guido Cavalcanti (1910), Pound entered a very strong claim for the powers of rhythm: "I believe in an ultimate and absolute rhythm as I believe in an absolute symbol or metaphor. The perception of the intellect is given in the word, that of the emotions in the cadence. It is only, then, in the perfect rhythm joined to the perfect word that the two-fold vision can be recorded."[18] This line

of speculation is continued in a way that explains Pound's later
handling of melopoeia:

> Rhythm is perhaps the most primal of all things known to us. It is basic
> in poetry and music mutually, their melodies depending on a variation on
> tone quality and of pitch respectively, as is commonly said, but if we look
> more closely we will see that music is, by further analysis, pure rhythm;
> rhythm and nothing else, for the variation of pitch is the variation in
> rhythms of the individual notes, and the harmony the blending of these
> varied rhythms. When we know more of overtones we will see that the
> tempo of every masterpiece is absolute, and is exactly set by some further
> law of rhythmic accord. Whence it should be possible to show that any
> given rhythm implies about it a complete musical form—fugue, sonata, I
> cannot say what form, but a form, perfect, complete. Ergo, the rhythm set
> in a line of poetry connotes its symphony, which, had we a little more skill,
> we could score for orchestra. *Sequitur*, or rather *inest*: the rhythm of any
> poetic line corresponds to emotion.
>
> It is the poet's business that this correspondence be exact, i.e., that it be
> the emotion which surrounds the thought expressed.[19]

The complex relation between absolute rhythm and poetic emotion can hardly be expressed by a simple *sequitur* or *inest*, and
Pound does not explain the connection. He evidently feels it
strongly, however, for he repeats the point in "Prolegomena"
(1912): "I believe in an 'absolute rhythm,' a rhythm, that is, in
poetry which corresponds exactly to the emotion or shade of emotion to be expressed. A man's rhythm must be interpretative, it will
be, therefore, in the end, his own, uncounterfeitable" (*LE*, p. 9).
Clearly, the operation of rhythm *takes time*, so that its effect cannot
present a complex object in an instant. On the other hand, the
"two-fold" effect of melopoeia, by furnishing a bridge between
consciousness and the universe and by reminding the reader of "the
most primal of all things known to us," may release the poet and
reader alike from the world of ordinary time and space.

Of phanopoeia, defined as "a casting of images upon the visual
imagination" (*LE*, p. 25), Pound says little that has not already
been said in his imagist statements. Image casting is a power of
words that relates more to their intellectual content than to their
charge of emotion, and in "How to Read" Pound pays less atten-

tion to phanopoeia than he does to melopoeia (one of his most enduring concerns) and to logopoeia. The "visual imagination" in his aesthetic is chiefly a matter of apprehending the shapes and colors of objects, and as such it is the faculty that is appealed to by the "clarity and directness" (*LE*, p. 33) that hold such a high place among imagist ideals.

"How to Read" does not mention the visionary possibilities of phanopoeia; the concentration there is strictly on the visual. But in Pound's handling of the term ten years earlier, the vision-seeing dimension is as prominent as the perception of physical shapes and colors. The three Cantos of 1917, subsequently rejected, are full of visions,[20] and they are parts of the poem that Pound thought of calling "Phanopoeia." In 1918, between definitions of "melopoeia" and "logopoeia" that sound much like the definitions in "How to Read," Pound offered the element that was to become phanopoeia: "Imagism, or poetry wherein the feelings of painting and sculpture are predominant (certain men move in phantasmagoria; the images of their gods, whole countrysides, stretches of hill land and forest, travel with them)."[21] And, in the set of poems that have kept the name "Phanopoeia," shapes and colors are used to evoke a mysterious experience of transfiguration:

> The wire-like bands of colour involute mount from
>   my fingers;
> I have wrapped the wind round your shoulders
> And the molten metal of your shoulders
>   bends into the turn of the wind,
> AOI!
> The whirling tissue of light
>   is woven and grows solid beneath us;
> The sea-clear sapphire of air, the sea-dark clarity,
>   stretches both sea-cliff and ocean.[22]

Just as melopoeia is not simply a matter of pleasing musical effects, phanopoeia is much more than the use of shapes and colors to describe physical objects. In both of these elements of poetry, as Pound defines and uses them, it is possible to register timeless moments of metamorphosis from the objective to the subjective and from the casual to the permanent.

Logopoeia, Pound says, "employs words not only for their direct meaning, but it takes count in a special way of habits of usage, of the context we *expect* to find with the word, its usual concomitants, of its known acceptances, and of ironical play. It holds the aesthetic content which is peculiarly the domain of verbal manifestation, and cannot possibly be contained in plastic or in music. It is the latest come, and perhaps most tricky and undependable mode" (*LE*, p. 25). The *logo* in Pound's term means "idea" as well as "word," so that "logopoeia" means "thought making" or "the poetry of thoughts." This aspect of poetry is most conspicuous in texts that are deliberately ambiguous for purposes of irony or humor. Elizabethan puns of the *color-collar-choler* variety, for example, depend on the audience's knowledge of many meanings of all three words; a composite total meaning is generated by the complex of references and connotations attached to each word. This is one more device that permits the expression of intellectual and emotional complexes in an instant; the richness of logopoeia makes it possible for a poet to say several different things, some of which may even be contradictory, at once.

"How to Read" is, I think, Pound's best critical work. With the triad of melopoeia, phanopoeia, and logopoeia, Pound illuminates the abundance and complexity of the devices by which language can be so highly charged that it effects an instantaneous presentation and seems thereby to transcend the limits and conditions of time.[23]

Pound continues, "All writing is built up of these three elements, plus 'architectonics' or 'the form of the whole'" (*LE*, p. 26). Regrettably, he does not pursue the problem of form, and such failure to talk much about anything but language is a serious flaw in Pound's formal and technical criticism. Another flaw is the omission of any thoroughgoing examination of the problem of genres. Prose is distinguished from poetry only because the language of prose is "much less highly charged"; and drama too is dismissed in terms of the charging of language: "The drama is a mixed art; it does not rely on the charge that can be put into the word, but calls on gesture and mimicry and 'impersonation' for assistance" (*LE*, pp. 26, 29). We have seen already that Pound's criticism of the novel tends to get away from technical and formal questions and to concentrate instead on social circumstances. For him, as for many other modern critics, literature is a problem of language and not much else. Since there are things besides words in drama, he must categorize it as a mixed art; a more comprehensive critic, like Aristotle, is able to consider drama as an organized whole of which language is one part. It is to such comprehensive critics that one must go for discussion of the "architectonics," for Pound stops far short of that question.

An undated note at the end of "How to Read" in *Literary Essays* says that the "argument of this essay is elaborated in the author's *A B C of Reading*" (*LE*, p. 40), but in that book there is very little that is not already adequately presented in "How to Read." At the same time, *A B C of Reading* does nothing to correct the deficiencies of "How to Read"—such failures as the lack of consideration given to important elements of poetry other than the language. For this "textbook" Pound adopts a rather pompous epigrammatic style, often with paragraphs only one sentence long separated by portentous-looking extra spaces. The style, to be sure, produces some memorable slogans—"Artists are the antennae of the race" or "More writers fail from lack of character than from lack of intelligence"[24]—but this approach does not facilitate the systematic development of the author's argument. As in "How to Read," the emphasis is all on the language of poetry. In his consideration of drama, Pound simply repeats the idea that it contains elements that are extraneous to the operation of language; and he modestly grants that he cannot say much about novels because he has never written one (*ABC*, pp. 76, 89). He says that "an epic is a poem containing history" and that Shakespeare's historical plays "form the true English EPOS" (*ABC*, pp. 46, 59); but that is all he has to say about the subject, perhaps because he thinks that criticism, like poetry, should consist only of "gists and piths" (*ABC*, p. 92).

Earlier, in connection with "In a Station of the Metro," it was seen that the suppression of verbs in a poem contributes to the effect of instantaneous presentation. Without the causal and chronological process of predication and without the explicit indication of time inherent in verbs by virtue of tense inflections,[25] the linguistic pattern, as experienced and as remembered, seems to take on a kind of timelessness, even though the apprehension of the pattern still takes time. (The shorter the poem, of course, the closer will the apprehension approach timelessness.)

Pound's grasp of the use of such grammatical effects seems to be chiefly intuitive, for there is no reference to them in either "How to Read" or *A B C of Reading*. In scattered places, however, he does suggest a conscious manipulation of grammatical distinctions. At one point in *Jefferson and/or Mussolini*, for example, he says:

> Again a little grammar or a little mediaeval scholarship would be useful. Albertus Magnus or Aquinas or some fusty old scribbler passed on an age-old distinction between the verb and the noun.
> The verb implies a time, a relation to time. Be Christian, go back to the newer part of your Bible. Be Catholic (not Anglo-Catholic), consider the "mystery of the incarnation."[26]

In his essay on Guido Cavalcanti, he displays the same sense of grammatical subtleties (and uses almost the same language and examples) when justifying his choice of certain readings in the corrupt text of the canzone "Donna mi priegha":

> I guessed right in stressing the difference between *Amore* (noun) and *Amare* (verb) in the first strophe. The philosophical difference is that a noun is a significant sound which makes no discrimination as to time. "Nomen est vox significativa, ad placitum, sine tempore, cuius nulla pars est significativa separate." The verb locates in time. "Verbum logice consideratum est quod consignificat tempus" (Albertus Magnus).
> The reader will see that the English version of St. John loses this philosophical or metaphysical shade in reading: "the word became flesh," for "verbum caro," etc.
>
> [LE, pp. 174–75][27]

Pound does take up again the question of rhythm and time in a "Treatise on Metrics" appended to *A B C of Reading*. Here he says, "Rhythm is a form cut into TIME, as a design is determined SPACE"

(*ABC*, p. 198). Conventional prosodic measurements, depending on a misconception of the basic unit of rhythm, simply do not apply to poetic language as it is spoken, chanted, or sung. Pound says that the "articulate sounds" of the language, with variable weights and duration that vary even more according to context, are "the medium wherewith the poem cuts his design in TIME." He accounts for failure in this department of poetry:

> If the poet hasn't a sense of time and of the different qualities of sound, this design will be clumsy and uninteresting just as a bad draughtsman's drawing will be without distinction.
> The bad draughtsman is bad because he does not perceive space and spatial relations, and cannot therefore deal with them.
> The writer of bad verse is a bore because he does not perceive time and time relations, and cannot therefore delimit them in an interesting manner, by means of longer and shorter, heavier and lighter syllables, and the varying qualities of sound inseparable from the words of his speech.
>
> [*ABC*, pp. 198–99]

But in a ten-page treatise Pound cannot give anything like a full examination to the complexities of prosody, which must include procedures for the measurement of quantity and quality of syllables, number of syllables or feet, and the interaction of syntactic articulations, prosodic patterns, and the arrangements of lines on a page.

A B C of Reading is Pound's last full book devoted to criticism, but it would be unjust to end an examination of his aesthetic ideas without looking briefly at some of the work he did after 1934. In the anthology *Confucius to Cummings* (1964), it is evident that he has modified some earlier judgments; Sophocles, for example, is elevated to a new position in the gallery of masters.[28] But it is also evident that the general principles of Pound's thought have changed hardly at all since *A B C of Reading*. He still thinks that "England's great, true, uneven epic is in the series of Shakespeare's 'Histories,' as distinct from literary imitations,"[29] and his rough differentiation of genres remains what it has been for thirty years: "Some distinction among the various kinds of poetry may eliminate gross miscomprehension. Lyric and epic have their own rights. If you define an epic as a 'poem including history' you admit elements improper to brief emotional utterance. Drama differs from poetry made to be sung or spoken by one person in that it is a text to be used in combination with human beings or puppets in action, gesticulating or quiet. The verbal manifest is not the whole show but can be or usually needs to be completed by movement and interplay."[30]

As with his social thought, then, Pound's technical and formal criticism can be seen as a complex of dialectical relations between kinds of time and timelessness. In his early imagist writings he controverted a traditional principle—that the verbal medium is necessarily subjugated by the temporal dimension—by trying to show that certain ways of handling the medium enable it to give at least the impression of timelessness. Thereafter he refined the general idea of imagist concentration and impact by analyzing poetry into three components—each of which, by charging language to the utmost degree, is capable of transcending temporal and spatial limits. But if poetry of a certain sort contains history, then it must bear some conditional relation to its own times and move with or against the zeitgeist. Such poetry may be said to express its time, just as all poetry expresses the character of its maker at a given time. It remains now for us to see how in his own poems Pound has realized his cultural and critical thought, which moves back and forth between temporal circumstances and timeless values.

PERSONAE

4 AND TIME

The whole of *Personae*—Ezra Pound's collection of shorter poems, first published in 1926, that finally became the *Collected Shorter Poems* of 1968—presents the image of a passionate modern man repeatedly visiting the past in order to recover cultural and personal values that are in danger of perishing. Many of the earlier, simpler poems in the book take up various aspects of the face of time; the flux of events appears as an "overflowing river . . . run mad" ("Paracelsus in Excelsis"[1]) and "quicksand" ("Her Monument, the Image Cut Thereon," *CSP*, p. 55). The figure of time-as-death is presented in various costumes. Death is called "that grey fencer" in "For E. McC." (*CSP*, p. 33); "Sir Death that deadly warrior" appears in "Planh for the Young English King" (*CSP*, p. 50); and in "Pan is Dead" the poet affirms that "Death was ever a churl" (*CSP*, p. 83). These phrases come from some of Pound's most melodramatic adaptations and original works, poems that T. S. Eliot is said to have called "touchingly incompetent."[2] The four lines that serve as the epigraph to *Lustra* (1916), however, provide an expression of the theme of mortality most simply and powerfully:

> *And the days are not full enough*
> *And the nights are not full enough*
> *And life slips by like a field mouse*
> > *Not shaking the grass.*

> [*CSP*, p. 90]³

One simple response to the spectacle of flux and mortality is the decision to eat, drink, and be merry—a policy articulated in "The Cloak" (*CSP*, p. 79), a poem of seduction. Another response is in "Troy," a variation of the convention of *ubi sunt*. The poem begins with a question to the city: "Whither . . . are your profits and your gilded shrines?" Only the powers of memory and art preserve the glories:

> *Time's tooth is into the lot, and war's, and fate's too.*
> *Envy has taken you all,*
> *Save your douth and your story.*

> [*CSP*, p. 183]

There are striking images of the horror of aging in "La Fraisne" (*CSP*, pp. 18–19) and "Piere Vidal Old" (*CSP*, pp. 44–46); and the suite "Impressions of François-Marie Arouet (de Voltaire)" rehearses most of the temporal themes handled in Pound's early verse. The first of these "impressions," "Phyllidula and the Spoils of Gouvernet," is a witty *ubi sunt*; the second, "To Madame du Châtelet," is a lament for the inevitable passing of the moment of love; and the third, "To Madame Lullin," affirms the strength of memory and art to withstand the destructive flux of events (*CSP*, pp. 185–86).

The painful comparison of present with past applies to cultures as well as to individuals. "O most unfortunate age!"—the conclusion of "To Formianus' Young Lady Friend" (*CSP*, p. 123)—is a familiar lament in an age that considers itself debased. In such a period one of the most saliently typical categories of literature adapts contemporary subjects to forms of plot and style derived from the myths and legends of better ages. Pound's "Tempora" (*CSP*, p. 121) is a minor member of a class of works dominated by

Man and Superman, Ulysses, and *Doktor Faustus.* The contrast between ages animates "Provincia Deserta," in which the poet gives
an account of a walking tour through Provence. "I have walked
there / thinking of old days," he says, recollecting the churches,
castles, and roads that are still rich in associations with kings and
their warriors and troubadours. After remembering some scattered
anecdotes of the region, the poet concludes:

> *That age is gone;*
> *Pieire de Maensac is gone*
> *I have walked over these roads;*
> *I have thought of them living.*

[*CSP*, pp. 131–33]

In his social and critical writings, as we have seen, Pound sets
forth strategies both for propagating values from the past and for
arresting the temporal movement of language so that the poem, by
seeming timeless, frees the reader from his limits of time and space.
This kind of struggle against time—the evils of which have been
seen in the poems just surveyed—is one of the grand themes of
Pound's poetry. He stresses various positive qualities that, combined with simple memory, may bring about the preservation of
values that would otherwise be buried by time. These positive
qualities, in ascending order of importance, are fame, magic, art,
and love.

In "Famam Librosque Cano," a Browningesque monologue
concerning the durability of poets' reputations, the poet imagines a
future in which his work is discovered on a bookstall by a shabby
old browser:

> *"Ah-eh! that strange rare name . . .*
> *Ah-eh! He must be rare if even I have not . . . "*
> *And lost mid-page*
> *Such age*
> *As his pardons the habit,*
> *He analyses form and thought to see*
> *How I 'scaped immortality.*

[*CSP*, p. 29]

This poem, originally in *A Lume Spento* (1908), is a reminder that Pound began his struggle against time by relying on the peculiar diction of an artifically archaic language. In early 1913, when he was twenty-seven years old, he wrote to Harriet Monroe, "God knows I wallowed in archaisms in my vealish years."[4] A volume of his earliest poetry was reissued recently with a foreword (dated 19 August 1964) in which Pound puts himself in the position of the old reader in "Famam Librosque Cano":

> A collection of stale creampuffs. "Chocolate creams, who hath forgotten you?["]
> At a time when Bill W. was perceiving the "Coroner's Children."
> As to why a reprint? No lessons to be learned save the depth of ignorance, or rather the superficiality of nonperception—neither eye nor ear. Ignorance that didn't know the meaning of "Wardour Street."[5]

A man in love with the past Pound may be, but the love is a matter of careful selection; ultimately (as will be seen later with regard to *The Cantos*) he is not in love with much of his own work at all. At the beginning of his career, however, he used archaism as a kind of time machine to transport himself into the past.

A poet's reputation, though perhaps more durable than physical beauty, is finally just as perishable; quiet early, Pound moved beyond the attitudes of "Famam Librosque Cano" to means other than reputation to thwart time. In much of his work there appears a fitful but recurrent belief in various sorts of incorporeal being. A few poems, notably "Ballad of the Goodly Fere" (*CSP*, pp. 47–48), state the orthodox Christian faith in the immortality of the soul. We have seen how the experience of something akin to metempsychosis is represented in "Histrion" (*ALS*, p. 108);[6] in several other poems such themes appear in contexts derived from the lore of many different systems of religion and philosophy. Much of Pound's thought is devoted to the practical working out of ideas in action and in time, and in Canto XIII Confucius is praised because, among other things, he "said nothing of the 'life after death.' "[7] But in his earliest poetry and in much of his subsequent work, Pound himself was preoccupied with mythic and mystical representations of the differences between mortality and immortality. In the "Note Precedent" that accompanied the early version of "La Fraisne," Pound said, "When the soul is exhausted in fire, then doth the spirit return unto its primal nature and there is upon it a great peace." In this mood the poet feels himself divided between his corporeal self and "a self aetherial" (*ALS*, p. 14). A good many of the early poems subsequently rejected from the canon of *Personae* have to do with reincarnation and other such mysteries that defy ordinary time; a few of the poems on magic, perhaps because they are not quite so bad as the very worst examples of this class, have survived with the poet's endorsement. [8]

In "Paracelsus in Excelsis" and "The Alchemist" (*CSP*, pp. 46, 86–87), the poet conducts an inquiry into certain superficial characteristics of necromantic art. This enterprise inevitably leads him across Yeats's path, as indicated by the title of the light poem "The Lake Isle" and by the reference to Oisin in "The Flame" (*CSP*, pp. 128, 64). [9] The latter poem describes an eternal state in which "time is shrivelled down to time's seed corn," a region suffused by "the clear light / Where time burns back about th' eternal embers."

Most of the magical poems discussed thus far are spoiled, I think, by a disagreeable atmosphere of fakery, a sense that the poet is capriciously manipulating the tawdry machinery of sorcery without really believing in what he is doing. A few poems do, however, present supernatural states of mind and being in a brilliant fashion. "Heather," which first appeared in 1915, presents a complex image of transfiguration:

> *The black panther treads at my side,*
> *And above my fingers*
> *There float the petal-like flames.*
>
> *The milk-white girls*
> *Unbend from the holly trees,*
> *And their snow-white leopard*
> *Watches to follow our trace.*

[*CSP*, p. 119]

Since this poem deals with some timeless state, it is impossible to describe its precise meaning in temporal terms. The state is clearly magical because the panther and the flames, potentially figures of terror, are here peacefully under control. The management of the otherworldly scene succeeds because Pound presents it in a matter-of-fact way with the feeling of "presentness" inherent in the present tense and the definite article.[10] The mysterious circumstances are simply present, and the poet presents them simply, with an effect of luminous phantasmagoria that goes beyond magic and myth.[11]

"Cantus Planus," first published in 1918, is a companion piece to "Heather" and uses a similar complex of metamorphic images:

> *The black panther lies under the rose tree*
> *And the fawns come to sniff at his sides:*
>
> > *Evoe, Evoe, Evoe Baccho, O*
> > ZAGREUS, Zagreus, *Zagreus,*
>
> *The black panther lies under his rose tree.*
> > ‖ *Hesper adest.   Hesper* ‖ *adest*
> > *Hesper* ‖ *adest.* ‖

[*CSP*, p. 248]

These lines were printed at the end of the *Personae* of 1926, perhaps as a "cantus" to link with *The Cantos*, which makes up the remainder of Pound's poetry. *Cantus planus* is the Medieval Latin name for what is now called "plainsong," the rhythmically free vocal music used in the early Christian church. For Pound's purposes it is important that the form is antique, musical, free, and religious. A turbulent agitation warps the surface of the poem—driving it first from English into Latin and Greek and then from intellectual language altogether into a zone of half-articulate cries and chants that require musical notation to supplement conventional punctuation.[12] In "Vorticism" Pound said that "there is a sort of poetry where music, sheer melody, seems as if it were just bursting into speech" (*GB*, p. 82). And in "Cantus Planus" he is working in a metamorphic border region—a mysterious zone between the objective and the subjective, between poetry and music.

"Cantus Planus" decocts many features of the intense emotional experiences that Pound frequently refers to in his earlier poetry and criticism.[13] He shifts the focus of the poem away from the English language and toward antique music.[14] "Cantus Planus" transcends physical and historical time, then, in two ways: the object imitated is a state of mystical consciousness, and the means of imitation is an anachronistic conjunction of languages and media that have seldom been joined in such a way before. "Heather" and "Cantus Planus," read at their simplest level, seem to celebrate the metamorphic hours of dawn and evening in terms and forms derived from archaic European religions—the same terms and forms that are travestied in "Ancient Music" to bemoan the coming of winter (which is, after all, another kind of temporal metamorphosis):

> Winter is icummen in,
> Lhude sing Goddamm,
> Raineth drop and staineth slop,
> And how the wind doth ramm!
>> Sing: Goddamm.

[CSP, p. 127]

In these poems and in several others—mostly lyric celebrations of love, spring, and morning—Pound struggles to retard the forward linear motion of time by returning to the past for techniques that implement the religious (or irreligious) observance of the cyclical movement of the days and seasons.

Again and again in *Collected Shorter Poems* the most conspicuous enterprise is an attempt at resurrection. In "Epilogue (to my five books containing mediaeval studies, experiments and translations)" the poet presents himself as one who has "laboured long in the tombs" (*CSP*, p. 267). The singer of "Villonaud for This Yule" is "wining the ghosts of yesteryear" (*CSP*, p. 24) in the sense of toasting them, of course, and perhaps also in the sense of bringing them back to life by stimulating them with wine and music. The note that precedes "Sestina: Altaforte" shows the poet trying to restore some of the luster to a tarnished reputation by promising to make a dead man speak:

> LOQUITUR: En *Bertrans de Born.*
> *Dante Alighieri put this man in hell for that*
> *he was a stirrer up of strife.*
> *Eccovi!*
> *Judge ye!*
> *Have I dug him up again?*
>
> [*CSP*, p. 42]

A similar theme of resurrection by the powers of love and art is registered in the line "The eyes of this dead lady speak to me," which is used in both "The Picture" and "Of Jacopo del Sellaio" (*CSP*, pp. 84–85), a matched pair of poems that concern the painting called *Venus Reclining*; the idea appears a third time (as "Les yeux d'une morte / M'ont salué") in "Dans un Omnibus de Londres" (*CSP*, p. 179). A related figure is registered in "Coda," a poem that could serve as an introduction to all of Pound's work:

> *O my songs,*
> *Why do you look so eagerly and so curiously*
>   *into people's faces,*
> *Will you find your lost dead among them?*
>
> [*CSP*, p. 113]

In this paradigm of Pound's struggle to recover the past, there is a realization of the personal themes handled earlier in such clumsy poems as "Histrion" and "On His Own Face in a Glass" (*CSP*, p. 49) and also of the theme of eternalizing poetry in all his boringly boastful "Come-my-song" poems and in "N. Y." (*CSP*, p. 74).

In most of Pound's love poems, the passage of physical time is explicitly countered by the timeless "hours" of erotic time. "A Virginal" ends with an image of trees in April and a transcendent splendor: "As white their bark, so white this lady's hours" (*CSP*, p. 83). The word "hour" is prominent in two other love poems in *Collected Shorter Poems*, both dating from 1911 and both having

Latin titles. "Erat Hora" is a dramatic lyric memorializing the fact that, no matter what else may happen, "one hour was sunlit" (*CSP*, p. 54), and "Horae Beatae Inscriptio" is a more rapturous expression of the same thought:

> *How will this beauty, when I am far hence,*
> *Sweep back upon me and engulf my mind!*
>
> *How will these hours, when we twain are gray,*
> *Turned in their sapphire tide, come flooding o'er us!*
>
> [CSP, p. 65]

Such a flow of tide of years is one of the commonest figures in Pound's poetry, and among the regular properties of his love poems is "Time" itself, in some manifestation, usually accompanied by images of water. One is reminded that the original sense of "tide" is "time" or "season." At times, as in "The Plunge" (*CSP*, p. 82), the tone is almost clownishly rhapsodic; at other times, as in "Stele," the poet turns the figure to witty use:

> *After years of continence*
> > *he hurled himself into a sea of six women.*
>
> [CSP, p. 199]

"Sub Mare," like the other love poems with Latin titles, successfully captures the effect of love on ordinary space and time:

> *It is, and is not, I am sane enough,*
> *Since you have come this place has hovered round me,*
> *This fabrication built of autumn roses,*
> *Then there's a goldish color, different.*
>
> *And one gropes in these things as delicate*
> *Algae reach up and out, beneath*
> *Pale slow green surgings of the underwave,*
> *'Mid these things older than the names they have,*
> *These things that are familiars of the god.*
>
> [CSP, p. 82]

"The House of Splendour" presents another phanopoeic account

of the powers of art and love together against the mortal limits of
life. The house is "out somewhere beyond the worldly ways." The
"ways and walls" of love replace the worldly ways and the walls of
time itself:

> *Here am I come perforce my love of her,*
> *Behold my adoration*
> *Maketh me clear, and there are powers in this*
> *Which, played on by the virtue of her soul,*
> *Break down the four-square walls of standing time.*
>
> [CSP, p. 63]

I have been dealing with certain themes—fame, magic, art, and
love—that dominate most of the shorter poems in *Collected Shorter
Poems*. I want now to trace the same themes, as instruments to
thwart the flux of time, in four larger masses of Pound's poetry.
These four—the "Rihaku" poems in *Cathay*, "Near Perigord,"
Homage to Sextus Propertius, and *Hugh Selwyn Mauberley*—differ
among themselves in many respects, needless to say, but they do
have several features in common. The principal voice in each belongs to a poet, usually minor or foreign. This typical masked voice
in each instance makes a series of attempts to recapture and preserve some lost value. The theme of loss and quest is essentially
fixed on an axis between love and death; at certain places the poles
shift to art and time, but the axis remains substantially the same.
The commonest conditions of the personae are disfavor, loneliness,
and exile, so that many of these poems are cast in various literary
modes of isolation: letters, soliloquies, farewells, memoirs, epi-
taphs, and meditations on death.

Such longer poems would seem at first glance to contradict the
principles of Pound's aesthetic of concentration, which is best realized in miniatures like "In a Station of the Metro" and "Coda."
Indeed, in much of his earlier criticism, he struggled with the difficult problem of reconciling imagist principles with the practice of
certain poets whose work he admired. He resisted the label of
"epic" for Dante's *Commedia* and assigned the work to other
genres, calling it "in a sense lyric, the tremendous lyric of the

subjective Dante" and also "a great mystery play, or better, a cycle of mystery plays."[15] The point is to defend the *Commedia* against charges of diffuseness, because presumably the effect of the perfect poem must be discharged in an instant of time. To make a case for concentration in so long a poem, Pound decided that the *"Divina Commedia* is a single elaborated metaphor of life."[16] Such a balance of economy and magnitude matters for Pound's own poetry, for soon after 1912 he seems to have grown tired of the limited possibilities of two- and three-line poems.

Pound tells us that "Rihaku" is a Japanese version of the name of Li Po, and it seems to me that he preserves an alien form for reasons that go beyond ignorance or stubbornness. Just as "Cathay" is a fanciful land quite remote from any real China, "Rihaku" is an effigy, and we see the real Li Po plain, if at all, only through several supervening layers of glass (languages, cultures, and interpreters). Li Po is concealed by an alias that is itself further obscured by the fragmentary work of a Japan-loving American with an Italian-sounding Spanish name whose notes have passed after his death to an Idaho-born cosmopolite living for a time in London.[17] The same strategic palimpsest of cultural layering and conflation of separate texts[18] occurs in much of Pound's work, notably *The Cantos*. It seems at times that Pound is by reflex unwilling to handle his materials, whether natural or cultural, at first hand; he much prefers to manipulate a complex of quasi personae speaking quasi translations. The procedure seems wholly laudable to me, but it should not be mistaken for something it is not; it is original poetry and not translation.[19] I take the risk of overworking this point because it is important to dissociate Pound from the responsibilities of translation. Thus disencumbered, he can be seen in the "Rihaku" poems at work on his customary themes in a refreshing new manner. In all of *Cathay* there are only a half-dozen exclamation points and not a single "O!"; the poems are written almost exclusively in declarative sentences in the present tense. It may be that Pound was too unfamiliar with the richness and subtleties of the Chinese originals to see anything but a very simple outline; even so, *Cathay* remains a model of clarity and economy.[20]

Rihaku in "The River Song" is aware of both the destructiveness of time and the uncertainty of his own profession, but he counters both modes of awareness with increased attention to his immediate surroundings and his own powerful art:

> *King So's terraced palace*
> > *is now but barren hill,*
> *But I draw pen on this barge*
> *Causing the five peaks to tremble,*
> *And I have joy in these words*
> > *like the joy of blue islands.*
> *(If glory could last forever*
> *Then the waters of Han would flow northward.)*
>
> *And I have moped in the Emperor's garden, awaiting*
> > *an order-to-write!*
> *I looked at the dragon-pond, with its*
> > *willow-colored water*
> *Just reflecting the sky's tinge,*
> *And heard the five-score nightingales aimlessly*
> > *singing.*

> [*CSP*, pp. 138–39]

In "The River-Merchant's Wife: A Letter" Rihaku uses what might be called the form of the "dramatic epistle" to demonstrate the power of love to withstand the passage of time. "Poem by the Bridge at Ten-Shin" departs from the positive note that concludes both "The River Song" and "The River-Merchant's Wife." Here the poet places himself in an ideal position—on a bridge in March —in a place and a time, that is, that give him a good view of the lines and circles left behind by metamorphic transitions of events:

> *March has come to the bridge head,*
> *Peach boughs and apricot boughs hang over a*
> > *thousand gates,*
> *At morning there are flowers to cut the heart,*
> *And evening drives them on the eastward-flowing waters.*
> *Petals are on the gone waters and on the going,*

> *And on the backswirling eddies,*
> *But today's men are not the men of the old days,*
> *Though they hang in the same way over the bridge-rail.*

The redundancy of "backswirling eddies" underlines the circular patterns of recurrence that mark natural events, in contrast to which the linear decline of human achievements is thrown into pronounced relief. The poet at the bridge in March sees the modern lords going forth to wars or pleasures, and his disdain for their vanity gives way to his emphatic admiration for the heroic figures of the past:

> *Night and day are given over to pleasure*
> *And they think it will last a thousand autumns,*
> > *Unwearying autumns.*
> *For them the yellow dogs howl portents in vain,*
> *And what are they compared to the lady Riokushu,*
> > *That was cause of hate!*
> *Who among them is a man like Han-rei*
> > *Who departed alone with his mistress,*
> *With her hair unbound, and he his own skiffsman!*
>
> [*CSP*, pp. 141–42]

Again and again in *Cathay* the relatively peaceful poetic surface is set against the turbulence of some kind of temporal transition. The predominant seasons are spring and autumn, and the predominant settings are bridges, gates, towers, stairs, windows, and frontiers— places that mediate between various sorts of human conditions. "The Jewel Stairs' Grievance," one of the shortest of the "Rihaku" poems, is an oblique but nonetheless dramatic treatment of the theme of lost love:

> *The jewelled steps are already quite white with dew,*
> *It is so late that the dew soaks my gauze stockings,*
> *And I let down the crystal curtain*
> *And watch the moon through the clear autumn.*
>
> [*CSP*, p. 142]

The bleakest poem in *Cathay* is also one of the best. I want to quote the whole of "Lament of the Frontier Guard" because it contains in its modest scope the full range of darker human emotions, stretching from the precise recording of "casualty figures" to an expansion of the immediate landscape to include all of the past and future:

> By the North Gate, the wind blows full of sand,
> Lonely from the beginning of time until now!
> Trees fall, the grass goes yellow with autumn.
> I climb the towers and towers
>   to watch out the barbarous land:
> Desolate castle, the sky, the wide desert.
> There is no wall left to this village.
> Bones white with a thousand frosts,
> High heaps, covered with trees and grass;
> Who brought this to pass?
> Who has brought the flaming imperial anger?
> Who has brought the army with drums and with
>   kettle-drums?
> Barbarous kings.
> A gracious spring, turned to blood-ravenous autumn,
> A turmoil of wars-men, spread over the middle kingdom,
> Three hundred and sixty thousand,
> And sorrow, sorrow like rain.
> Sorrow to go, and sorrow, sorrow returning.
> Desolate, desolate fields,
> And no children of warfare upon them,
>   No longer the men for offence and defence.
> Ah, how shall you know the dreary sorrow at the
>   North Gate,
> With Rihoku's name forgotten,
> And we guardsmen fed to the tigers.

[*CSP*, p. 143]

"Exile's Letter" is a grand memoir spoken by Rihaku in his own voice, as is the case in "Poem by the Bridge at Ten-Shin." It recounts the pleasant friendship between the poet and "So-Kin of Rakuyo, ancient friend, Chancellor of Gen." The memories include hard journeys and good parties:

> *Pleasure lasting, with courtezans, going and coming*
>   *without hindrance,*
> *With the willow flakes falling like snow,*
> *And the vermilioned girls getting drunk about sunset,*
> *And the water, a hundred feet deep, reflecting*
>   *green eyebrows*
> *—Eyebrows painted green are a fine sight in young*
>   *moonlight,*
> *Gracefully painted—*
> *And the girls singing back at each other,*
> *Dancing in transparent brocade,*
> *And the wind lifting the song, and interrupting it,*
> *Tossing it up under the clouds.*
>   *And all this comes to an end.*
>   *And is not again to be met with.*
>
>   [*CSP*, p. 146]

The technique displayed here exactly suits a persona who is himself a master poet. The memory is like the courtesans who dominate it, "going and coming without hindrance." The poet's mind moves in a comic pattern from courtesans to willow flakes and back to courtesans, then to water, back again to courtesans, then to the wind. The recollections are passed from one present participle to the next, all loosely articulated along a polysyndetic string of "and's" woven in long sentences and long lines. With the reference to the wind, however, the tone modulates and the rhythm shifts. The line is substantially indented, the present tense is introduced, and the verdict and sentence of time are recorded in words of one syllable: "And all this comes to an end." This letter, like that of the river merchant's wife, does not end at the climactic expression of feeling. The writer moves on to a few items of gossip ("I went up to the court for examination"), reflects again on things that do or do not have ends, and concludes on a note that balances domesticity and meditation:

> What is the use of talking, and there is no end
>   of talking,
> There is no end of things in the heart.
> I call in the boy,
> Have him sit on his knees here
>   To seal this,
> And send it a thousand miles, thinking.

[CSP, p. 146]

The poet's thought, it is clear, revolves the problem of aesthetic and ethical meditation between conditions of time and timelessness: "All this comes to an end" and "There is no end of things in the heart."

Cathay appeared in the spring of 1915; in December of that year, Poetry published two of Pound's most interesting poems, "Villanelle: The Psychological Hour" and "Near Perigord." The poems are quite different in many respects, but they are both notes on one problem: the impossibility of capturing time, whether past or present.

"Villanelle: The Psychological Hour" is not a villanelle at all; it is three short considerations of personal disappointment and social failure. The title seems to be an expansion of the phrase "psychological moment" that by 1915 had become perverted into English journalese for "the proper time."[21] The speaker is Pound himself, identified by name in the third section. (Such a piercing of the artificial persona takes place also in the seventh section of "Moeurs Contemporaines"—CSP, p. 200.)

The fragmented "villanelle" is about failure with respect to the present; "Near Perigord" is about ignorance with respect to the past. Here the poet's struggle to find out the truth about one small part of Bertrans de Born's life and work is a model of the larger struggle of art to comprehend the past and preserve the present. Bertrans's "Dompna pois de me no'us cal"[22] is ostensibly a poem in which the poet, unable to win the Lady Maent, takes notable traits from other ladies in the region to make up a "borrowed" lady. There is the possibility that the poem is actually an instrument of political strategy designed to stir up strife among the lords whose wives contribute traits to the composite lady. The first part of "Near Perigord" rehearses the known facts but ends only with a handful of questions. The second part begins with the abrupt technical note, "End fact. Try fiction," and here the poet imagines a series of dramatic scenes involving Bertrans himself and some friends who discuss his case (already something of a mystery even to his contemporaries), but again the search is unsuccessful. In the third part of the poem, Bertrans himself seems to be speaking in the context of 1915, exactly 700 years after his death. The style in this part is a pronounced departure from the idiom of the first two parts. Bertrans is less emphatic and fulsome than any of his own poems were; his manner is uncertain, elliptical, subject to frequent distractions and interruptions. He ends by describing the lady as a permanent mystery:

> *There shut up in his castle, Tairiran's,*
> *She who had nor ears nor tongue save in her hands,*
> *Gone—ah, gone—untouched, unreachable!*
> *She who could never live save through one person,*
> *She who could never speak save to one person,*
> *And all the rest of her a shifting change,*
> *A broken bundle of mirrors...!*

[*CSP*, pp. 171–77]

The love was lost and the record of it has perished. Except as Maent lived through the medium of the love and art of "one person" (Bertrans himself), she is nothing but the ambiguous occasion for endless speculation, like everything else in the past. "Near Perigord" begins by asking "What went on?" and ends with a much more complex problem: What is the meaning of the fact that one cannot determine what went on? Maent loved, therefore she was; otherwise she is absolutely dead and gone, and not even the durable monuments of art can withstand decay. All of the mirrors are broken; the sum of the fragmented reflections does not equal the sum of her being. The poem ends on this strange note, and the punctuation corresponds in strangeness. Points of ellipse suggest inconclusive uncertainty, but the exclamation point has precisely the opposite effect, as though saying, "And that, for better or worse, is all there is to it."

By the end of 1915, Pound was in command of a polyphonic collection of voices, but at the same time he was taking up increasingly difficult themes of failure and disappointment that imposed on him a modesty that seems quite remote from his earlier attitudes. "The Psychological Hour" and "Near Perigord" register two versions of a man's failure to overcome time. Both poems contain three parts, each shorter than the one before; both end by concentrating on a figure behind a persona, "Bertrans himself" and "Pound." Both are miniature tragedies of loss: loss of love or friendship, loss of time, and ultimately the loss of poetry as an efficient tool for digging up the past. It is the triumph of both poems, I think, to turn the failure of poetry itself into a subject for poetry. Subsequently, between 1916 and 1920, Pound kept up his search for the means of resurrecting the past—both his own and that of human culture—and again the instruments that he tried out were personae who are minor poets: the real Sextus Propertius and the fictional Hugh Selwyn Mauberley.

Pound's homage to Propertius begins with a paraphrase of Propertius' homage to his own literary ancestors: "Shades of Callimachus, Coan ghosts of Philetas" (*CSP*, p. 225). Propertius invokes also "a young Muse with loves clustered about her" to assist in his defense of competent personal poetry against the bombast of public rhetoric:

> *Annalists will continue to record Roman reputations,*
> *Celebrities from the Trans-Caucasus will belaud*
>   *Roman celebrities*
> *And expound the distensions of Empire,*
> *But for something to read in normal circumstances?*

Reviewing the power of poetry to keep things from perishing, he begins in mockery but ends with a serious claim for his art:

Small talk O Ilion, and O Troad
            twice taken by Oetian gods,
If Homer had not stated your case!
. . . .
Happy who are mentioned in my pamphlets,
        the songs shall be a fine tomb-stone over
            their beauty.
        But against this?
Neither expensive pyramids scraping the stars in
        their route,
Nor houses modelled upon that of Jove in East Elis,
Nor the monumental effigies of Mausolus,
            are a complete elucidation of death.
Flame burns, rain sinks into the cracks
And they all go to rack ruin beneath the thud
        of the years.
Stands genius a deathless adornment,
        a name not to be worn out with the years.

[*CSP*, pp. 225–27]

The first part of the "Homage" is a microcosm of the whole poem, and there is little in the remainder but a repetition of Latinate elaborations, descriptions of the pleasures and disappointments of love, and affirmations of the strength of true poetry against time. The poet produces lyrics because of immediate erotic inspiration— "My genius is no more than a girl" (*CSP*, p. 234)—and aware that "small talk comes from small bones" (*CSP*, p. 236), he seizes the present moment exuberantly. The drift of the poem is comic, for the poet seems convinced that the horror of death and vanities of daily life are adequately offset by his art and love. He exaggerates, obviously, but the fictions are gallant and courageous; the impotence of time to bring about any real damage is the theme on which Propertius is most eloquent. In a sense the "Homage" is a poem about poetry; and it ends as it began, with an act of respect to the ancient brotherhood of poets:

> *Varro sang Jason's expedition,*
>   *Varro, of his great passion Leucadia,*
> *There is a song in the parchment; Catullus the highly*
>   *indecorous,*
> *Of Lesbia, known above Helen;*
> *And in the dyed pages of Calvus,*
>   *Calvus mourning Quintilia,*
> *And but now Gallus had sung Lycoris.*
>   *Fair, fairest Lycoris—*
> *The waters of Styx poured over the wound:*
> *And now Propertius of Cynthia, taking his stand*
>   *among these.*
>
> [*CSP*, p. 247]

The circumstances of Pound's personae are seldom happy: Propertius is conscious of Cynthia's fundamental fickleness, Rihaku writes in exile, Bertrans is suffering in hell; yet with all these figures Pound affirms somehow the positive qualities of love and art, which provide at least the temporary illusion of peace. The poet finds that works of art still live, that the eyes of dead ladies can speak; and in these experiences he finds that good human qualities endure because of love.

No feature of Pound's work is more prominent than the emphasis on the conviction that things must live: they must move, grow, and renew themselves. Languages must be kept alive, and the record of great artists must not be allowed to perish. The forces of memory, culture, art, and love all work to keep the valuable qualities of the past magically alive. Occasionally, Pound's insistence on these qualities waxes hysterical, as in his claims for the primacy of the present as "vortex": "All experience rushes into this vortex. All the energized past, all the past that is living and worthy to live. ALL MOMENTUM, which is the past bearing upon us, RACE, RACE-MEMORY, instinct charging the PLACID, NON-ENERGIZED FUTURE."[23] Many years later, in a very different mood, Pound discovered in a mystical vision that it is not vanity "to have gathered from the air a live tradition" (Canto LXXXI—*C*, p. 522), and

the key word here is "live." Such forms of rebirth and resurrection constitute the large pattern of comedy that informs most of
Pound's major works. Only *Hugh Selwyn Mauberley* departs in any
significant way from the pattern.

Hugh Selwyn Mauberley is about separation—variously mani-
fested as exile, isolation, obliviousness, callousness, and death. A
minor man of letters, Mauberley is ineffective in his sporadic efforts to seize the present or hold on to the past; none of the strategies—fame, memory, energy, art, love, wit—that serve Rihaku,
Bertrans, and Propertius will work for Mauberley. The sequence is
like a cemetery, with each cell containing a simple or compound
corpse. The subtitle "Life and Contacts" is twice ironic, for the true
subjects of the poem are death and separation.

The opening "E. P. Ode" is a condensed summary of the aspects
of time that appear in Pound's major cultural and critical texts.
Mauberley was born "out of date" and his ambitions were "out of
key with his time"; the zeitgeist was not congenial to his efforts to
resuscitate the art of poetry, which was "dead." Mauberley's unsuccessful efforts are registered in a quick series of metaphors:
opposing the zeitgeist and the gods ("Capaneus"), he is even duped
into opposing his own self-interest ("trout for factitious bait"). He
wastes his time, in several senses of "waste" and "time." Hypno-
tized by the "elegance of Circe's hair," he ignores her evil effect;
such elegance eclipses the mottoes on sundials—reminders like
tempus fugit. Time—the "march of events"—passes him by and
leaves him as dead as his art.

The second section of the poem examines the age itself and its
demands for inferior poetry. There are hints here that Mauberley's
alternatives are not much better than what the age demanded, a
"mould in plaster, / Made with no loss of time." "An Attic grace,"
"the obscure reveries / Of the inward gaze," and "the classics in
paraphrase" are remote, diluted debasements of classical ideals; the
expressions sound like clippings from bad book reviews. The running contrast between the demands of the age and the ideals of the
poet continues in the third section of the poem, where modern
developments are set against the imagined greatness of the past.

Again, however, irony deflects the directness of the contrast. To mock the present, the poet goes into the distant past to borrow heroic phrases from Pindar. (We know from letters that, for Pound, Pindar is not a representative of the greatness of antiquity but rather, as Pound said in 1916, "the prize wind-bag of all ages."[24]) It is vain to attack the tawdry cheapness of today with an equally tawdry cheapness from the past.

A strange modulation takes place in the next two sections of the poem. Instead of writing a burlesque of Pindaric patriotic bombast, the poet presents a pointed refutation of Horatian patriotic bombast. The departure from the tone and attitude of the foregoing sections is so pronounced that it is difficult to think that these sections are spoken by Mauberley or the ineffectual "E. P."; the voice sounds more like Ezra Pound's. The poet abandons the mannered sculpture of rhymed quatrains and such trifles as the lost "mousseline of Cos" to turn his passionate attention on the recent European war in which men (not gods and not heroes) died "pro patria, non 'dulce' non 'et decor.'" The shift in tone is remarkable; the poem simply says that Horace's slogan is false. The fifth section of *Hugh Selwyn Mauberley* is a moving epitaph for a generation and a civilization:

> There died a myriad,
> And of the best, among them,
> For an old bitch gone in the teeth,
> For a botched civilization.
>
> Charm, smiling at the good mouth,
> Quick eyes gone under earth's lid,
>
> For two gross of broken statues,
> For a few thousand battered books.

[*CSP*, pp. 205–208]

That is unanswerable. Although Pound did not fight in the war, he wrote a better poem about it than any of the combatants. Compared to Pound's lines, Wilfred Owen's "Dulce et Decorum Est" (probably written before *Hugh Selwyn Mauberley* but not published until 1921) is rather pale. Owen's rhyme of "glory" and "mori" points the contrast too smartly, and calling Horace's line "the old Lie" is much less telling than Pound's outright enactment of denial.

"Quick eyes"—recalling the eyes at the center of such earlier poems as "The Picture," "Of Jacopo del Sellaio," "Dans un Omnibus de Londres," and "Pagani's, November 8"—modulate into the sixth section of the poem, "Yeux Glauques." Here the poet looks back through the eyes of a dead lady to the time, sixty or seventy years earlier, when the Pre-Raphaelites were at work. This section inaugurates a lengthy examination of the lives of British artists, past and present. In one quatrain the poet relates the dead model to her own day, to the future, and to the past—a multiplicity of signification helped by the ambiguity of "still":

> *The Burne-Jones cartons*
> *Have preserved her eyes;*
> *Still, at the Tate, they teach*
> *Cophetua to rhapsodize.*

[*CSP*, p. 209]

Among images of a grotesquely preserved past—"pickled foetuses and bottled bones"—the poet hears the talk of M. Verog, who remembers the Decadents—some of whom were themselves preserved in alcohol, if not in art. "Brennbaum" presents a character who is very nearly another pickled foetus; at any rate he displays a combination of immaturity and deadness. As Verog is "out of step with the decade" and "detached from his contemporaries," Brennbaum is out of touch with his own heritage; and both men foreshadow what might become of Mauberley. No help comes from Mr. Nixon (in the ninth section of the poem) because a coffin of total commercialism has shut him off from the past of his own culture. His memories of his youth are strictly matters of money; he is a null and a nullifier (as his name suggests), and his advice, like that of "a friend of Bloughram's," ends on a note of negation: "There's nothing in it" (*CSP*, p. 212).

The next three sections of *Hugh Selwyn Mauberley* are in the present tense. "The stylist" has escaped from the world's welter to a run-down country dwelling. The figure here may not be dead, but it is doubtful that his life approaches an ideal condition. The poem moves to a quick sketch of a woman whose vital instincts have died—a kind of death economically recorded in the rhyme yoking of "feeling" and "Ealing." In the twelfth section, after a portrait of an empty lady, the poem returns to the contrast between the tawdry present and the many-layered past:

> *Conduct, on the other hand, the soul*
> *"Which the highest cultures have nourished"*
> *To Fleet St. where*
> *Dr. Johnson flourished;*
>
> *Beside this thoroughfare*
> *The sale of half-hose has*
> *Long since superseded the cultivation*
> *Of Pierian roses.*
>
> [CSP, p. 214]

In the section immediately succeeding this ludicrous rhyme, the poem offers a very different kind of rose, borrowing from the living past Waller's "Go, Lovely Rose" as a model for the "Envoi." Having inspected a gallery of corpses, the poet returns to his old promises of love and art that can stand against time. The lady's graces "give / Life to the moment"; the poet would prolong their life in "magic amber" so that they could brave time. In portentous italics the poet looks forward to a day

> *When our two dusts with Waller's shall be laid,*
> *Siftings on siftings in oblivion,*
> *Till change hath broken down*
> *All things save Beauty alone.*
>
> [CSP, p. 215]

This deceptive conclusion (dated 1919) is followed by a five-part codicil called "Mauberley 1920" in which themes already stated are developed in a freer manner. The relation between the main poem and the codicil is unclear,[25] but such ambiguity of structure is itself a clue to the meaning of the poem. The work as a whole attacks a complex problem of failure, and there is no simple way to solve such a problem. Many styles, languages, tenses, persons, and moods are needed to rotate the three-dimensional knot of puzzles so that all of it can be considered. The antique affirmation of the "Envoi" could end the poem, but that solution would be too pat. The "Envoi," though lovely indeed, represents a retreat down Wardour Street into the imaginary past, and the noble endorsement of Beauty with a capital *B* in italics cannot convincingly stand up in a context in which art is dead and civilization botched. The 1920 codicil seems designed to alter the comic form of the 1919 testament so that the materials are shaped anew.

In "Near Perigord" and "Villanelle: The Psychological Hour" the obscurity of motives precludes the presentation of a smoothly finished work. In many poems written between 1915 and 1920, Pound turns away from the representation of action, success, and love; he deals instead with fragmented records of apathy, failure, ignorance, blindness, loss, and rejection. The powers of poetry are increasingly weak against the evil flux of time. With these themes to express, Pound struggles more and more with techniques of incomplete elaboration and with poetic surfaces that reflect an imperfect world imperfectly. The personae of Rihaku and Propertius maintain a residual confidence in the powers of love and art, but no such confidence animates the rather macerated "Envoi" of *Hugh Selwyn Mauberley*. This poem turns out to be no more a proper *envoi* than "The Psychological Hour" is a proper villanelle. The symmetrical shapes and smooth surfaces attributed to Rihaku and Propertius are gradually displaced by sequences of fragments deliberately articulated in awkward, ambiguous ways. The art is not a matter of imposing ordered forms on chaotic matter or of drawing distinct outlines for a subject in flux.

If such imperfect representations are faithful, then paradoxically the reflection is not fragmentary but complete. It seems that "Mauberley" deliberately disturbs the comic assurance of the end of *Hugh Selwyn Mauberley*. "Medallion," the closing section of the postscript, recalls the poet's claim in the "Envoi" to construct a monument of love and beauty that will brave time. But here the lady is not really present, nor is her image rendered in some mode of classic art. Her eyes—not even as lively as the painted gaze in "Yeux Glauques"—at the end "turn topaz." However precious or beautiful, topaz is still a dead stone, and its image, perhaps an inappropriate color for living eyes, is a proper conclusion for an "overblotted / Series / Of intermittences" (*CSP*, p. 221). The eyes of a dead lady speak, but the mechanism is a sort of tawdry ventriloquism, and the message is not one of love or the power of art to preserve love's image.

Pound's poetry began with misguided gestures of thematic and technical homage to the past. Dissatisfaction with archaisms and artificial poses soon led him to adopt an aesthetic of renovation and concentration designed to preserve the human values of the past and present without destroying them in the process. The first manifestations of this policy were perfect but limited in scope and length. Gradually, he attempted a wide range of techniques and attitudes, all directed toward the resuscitation of an art moribund if not certifiably dead. He mastered a larger array of voices and characters than almost any other modern poet, but at times he published poems so awkwardly sentimental that not even the most charitable partisan can find anything of value in them. But there were also times when he wrote poems of enduring power that succeed as acts of homage to his elders and stand as monuments to his own great gifts.

POUND'S
5 RECORD OF STRUGGLE

The title of *Drafts & Fragments of Cantos CX–CXVII* (1969) confirmed the tentative status of Ezra Pound's largest poetic undertaking. The poem is unfinished; such parts as have been published are fragmentary. The earliest published experiments, dating back to 1917, were jettisoned before the first whole book of drafts came out in 1925. Two Cantos, LXXII and LXXIII, are missing almost entirely, and accounts of their whereabouts and features vary considerably.[1] Forty-one lines, labeled "Canto Proceeding (72 Circa)" when published in a magazine in 1942, appear with a few changes as "Addendum for Canto C" in *Drafts & Fragments*.[2] On the next page of that book, ten other lines appear in such a way that it is not clear whether they are also part of the "Addendum." They appeared first in a letter dated 12 March 1940 with the designation "lines from a new Canto—or rather for a new Canto," and their heading reads, "Lines to go into Canto 72 or somewhere."[3]

If such external features as title and numbering of parts are bewildering, the poem itself seems to go beyond the scale of human understanding. No literary work is more obscure or difficult. There seems to be no continuous dramatic or narrative plot. Characters, many of whom the reader has never heard of before, surface and submerge in patterns that defy analysis. A good deal of the language is not modern English, and some of the things on the page are not verbal language of any sort. The poem is full of mistakes of fact and spelling. Some of the racist ideas expressed (and presumably espoused) by the poet are as repulsive as almost anything in literature. These difficulties have stimulated a great deal of critical and scholarly labor designed to translate foreign passages and explain obscure allusions. Beyond such explication of details, there have been attempts to elucidate the form of the whole. These efforts ordinarily involve seeing *The Cantos* qua something else—an odyssey, a Dantean *commedia*, a fugue, a fresco, a gallery of statues, a conversation, a nightmare—but it seems to me that none of these explanations offers a wholly satisfactory account of the whole poem as we now possess it.

Pound himself was of no real help. Many of his letters and critical writings contain material that may directly or indirectly explain the source, form, or purpose of a given poem, but early on, he drew a definite line on the matter of explanation. In a preface to *A Quinzaine for This Yule* (1908), signed with the pseudonym "Weston St. Llewmys," he defended the integrity of his work:

> Beauty should never be presented explained. It is Marvel and Wonder, and in art we should find first these doors—Marvel and Wonder—and, coming through them, a slow understanding (slow even though it be a succession of lightning understandings and perceptions) as of a figure in mist, that still and ever gives to each one his own right of believing, each after his own creed and fashion.
>
> Always the desire to know and to understand more deeply must precede any reception of beauty. Without holy curiosity and awe none find her, and woe to that artist whose work wears its "heart on its sleeve."[4]

Nor is this simply the temporary petulance of a youngster fresh out of graduate school and sick of philology, for Pound repeats his stubborn claims many years later in the foreword (dated 20 October 1966) to *Selected Cantos*: "I have made these selections to indicate main elements in the Cantos. To the specialist the task of explaining them. As Jung says: 'Being essentially the instrument of his work he (the artist) is subordinate to it and we have no reason for expecting him to interpret it for us. He has done the best that is in him by giving it form and he must leave interpretation to others and to the future.' "⁵ Pound then says that the "best introduction to the Cantos" might be some lines from a largely rejected earlier draft of a Canto that he dates 1912, although it did not appear until 1917. (He refers the reader to a reprinting of the poem in the fiftieth-anniversary issue of *Poetry*, and I assume that he was confusing the date of the poem with the date of the founding of that magazine. On the other hand, 1912 could easily be the correct date for the draft, because Pound has been quoted by one interviewer as saying, "I began the *Cantos* about 1904, I suppose."⁶)

Most critics looking for a way into *The Cantos* have seized on some rather widely scattered remarks as hints of the form of the poem. A favorite passage is in a letter that Pound wrote to his father in 1927, giving an exegesis of some details of Canto XX and suggesting the main form:

Afraid the whole damn poem is rather obscure, especially in fragments. Have I ever given you outline of the main scheme:::or whatever it is?

1. Rather like, or unlike subject and response and counter subject in fugue.

A. A. Live man goes down into world of Dead

C. B. The "repeat in history"

B. C. The "magic moment" or moment of metamorphosis, bust thru from quotidien into "divine or permanent world." Gods, etc.

[*Ltrs*, p. 210]

There is less assistance than confusion here. The force of the remarks is vitiated by the puzzlement obvious in "whatever it is" and "like, or unlike." No one has explained why the *C* comes before the *B* in the outline (unless there is a mistake in D. D. Paige's transcription). In any event, with no more guidance than Pound offers here, it is extremely difficult to align his three elements with the parts of a fugue.

The author of *A B C of Economics* and *A B C of Reading*, continually explaining things to others, was in the habit of using alphabetical diagrams. Yeats's "A Packet for Ezra Pound," included in *A*

Vision in 1928, suggests another outline, this time in terms of painting instead of music:

[Pound] has scribbled on the back of another envelope certain sets of letters that represent emotions or archetypal events—I cannot find any adequate definition—ABCD and then JKLM, and then each set of letters repeated, and then a new element XYZ, then certain letters that never recur, and then all sorts of combinations of XYZ and JKLM and ABCD and DCBA, and all set whirling together. He has shown me upon the wall a photograph of a Cosimo Tura decoration in three compartments, in the upper the Triumph of Love and the Triumph of Chastity, in the middle Zodiacal signs, and in the lower certain events in Cosimo Tura's day. The Descent and the Metamorphosis—ABCD and JKLM—his fixed elements, took the place of the Zodiac, the archetypal persons—XYZ—that of the Triumphs, and certain modern events—his letters that do not recur—that of those events in Cosimo Tura's day.[7]

These are probably the words that Pound has in mind when he says in a letter, "God damn Yeats' bloody paragraph." In this letter of February 1939 he also says, "Done more to prevent people reading Cantos for what is *on the page* than any other one smoke screen" (*Ltrs*, p. 321). He adds:

There is *no intentional* obscurity.[8] There is condensation to maximum attainable. It is impossible to make the deep as quickly comprehensible as the shallow.

The order of words and sounds *ought* to induce the proper reading; proper tone of voice, etc., but can *not* redeem fools from idiocy, etc. If the goddam violin string is not tense, no amount of bowing will help the player. And *so* forth.

As to the *form* of The Cantos: all I can say or pray is: *wait* till it's there. I mean wait till I get 'em written and then if it don't show, I will start exegesis. I haven't an Aquinas-map; Aquinas *not* valid now.

[*Ltrs*, pp. 322–23]

And two paragraphs in *Guide to Kulchur* make the poem sound much clearer than it seems *on the page*:

There is no mystery about the Cantos, they are the tale of the tribe—give Rudyard credit for his use of the phrase. No one has claimed that the Malatesta cantos are obscure. They are openly volitionist, establishing, I think clearly, the effect of the factive personality, Sigismundo, an entire man. The founding of the Monte dei Paschi as the second episode has its importance. There we find the discovery, or at any rate the establishment, of the true bases of credit, to wit the abundance of nature and the responsibility of the whole people.

As history becomes better understood I think this emphasis will become steadily more intelligible to the general reader.[9]

Earlier, in a letter to John Drummond, Pound said of *The Cantos*, "Best div. prob. the permanent, the recurrent, the casual" (*Ltrs*, p. 239)—a triad that roughly corresponds to the divisions along musical lines suggested in the letter to his father and those along graphic lines suggested by Yeats's account of Pound's informal diagram. Dantean parallels are obvious; Pound said in 1944 that he had schooled himself for forty years "to write an epic poem which begins 'In the Dark Forest,' crosses the Purgatory of human error, and ends in the light, 'fra i maestri di color che sanno.' "[10] The "forty years" accords with Pound's assertion that he began *The Cantos* in 1904, but the word *epic* introduces an inconsistency. He argued in *The Spirit of Romance*, it should be remembered, that Dante's *Commedia* is anything but epic.[11] In a letter of 7 May 1924, he repeated the same point with regard to his own poem: "Do recall that the title of that book is 'A DRAFT of 16 Cantos for a poem of some length.' " He was upbraiding the publisher William Bird about the advertisements for the forthcoming publication of the first book of Cantos; he went on, "If you will stick to that you will produce something of gtr. val. to collectors. Also it ain't an epic. It's part of a long poem" (*Ltrs*, p. 189).

The poem *is* long—more than 800 pages; that much at least is clear. Everything else about it remains unclear. The meaning of each part is hard to determine, the connections between some parts appear capricious, and the form of the whole seems to be incomprehensible. Many brave critics have provided notes that elucidate individual passages, but no one has succeeded in showing exactly how and why each part relates to each other part and to the whole. Efforts to work out parallels between *The Cantos* and other works have sooner or later broken down. Some critics seem willing to toil with tons of earth in hopes of coming up with one or two nugget-like allusions, analogues, or sources. These labors are, of course, necessary and valuable, but at present their net result—particularly in the chauvinist journal *Paideuma*—has been to make *The Cantos* look like a very dull poem indeed.

There are a few obvious points that should be repeated about the poem. It gave Pound a good deal of trouble all along; it took him at least ten years to get its beginning into shape, after several false starts. Much of it remains a "draft," and with such a bulk of material, any considerable revision was largely out of the question. On the whole, the poet averaged a little over two Cantos a year for more than fifty years.

Guy Davenport, who interviewed Pound in the summer of 1953, reports among other things that the poet "finds his *Paradiso* the most difficult part of the poem to write."[12] In 1962 Pound told another interviewer, "It is difficult to write a paradiso when all the superficial indications are that you ought to write an apocalypse. It is obviously much easier to find inhabitants for an inferno or even a purgatorio. I am trying to collect the record of the top flights of the mind. I might have done better to put Agassiz on top instead of Confucius." And when asked in the same interview, "Are you more or less stuck?" Pound gave an answer that comes closer than any other statement to a full expression of the impulse and design of his poem:

Okay, I am stuck. The question is, am I dead, as Messrs. A. B. C. might wish? In case I conk out, this is provisionally what I have to do: I must clarify obscurities; I must make clearer definite ideas or dissociations. I must find a verbal formula to combat the rise of brutality—the principle of order versus the split atom. There was a man in the bughouse, by the way, who insisted that the atom had never been split.

An epic is a poem containing history. The modern mind contains heteroclite elements. The past epos has succeeded when all or a great many of the answers were assumed, at least between author and audience, or a great mass of audience. The attempt in an experimental age is therefore rash. Do you know the story: "What are you drawing, Johnny?"

"God!"

"But nobody knows what He looks like."

"They will when I get through!"

That confidence is no longer obtainable.

There are epic subjects. The struggle for individual rights is an epic subject, consecutive from jury trial in Athens to Anselm versus William Rufus, to the murder of Becket and to Coke and through John Adams.

Then the struggle appears to come up against a block. The nature of sovereignty is epic matter, though it may be a bit obscured by circumstance. Some of this *can* be traced, pointed; obviously it has to be condensed to get into the form. The nature of the individual, the heteroclite contents of contemporary consciousness. It's the fight for light versus subconsciousness; it demands obscurities and penumbras. A lot of contemporary writing avoids inconvenient areas of the subject.

I am writing to resist the view that Europe and civilisation [*sic*] is going to Hell. If I am being "crucified for an idea"—that is, the coherent idea around which my muddles accumulated—it is probably the idea that European culture ought to survive, that the best qualities of it ought to survive along with whatever other cultures, in whatever universality. Against the propaganda of terror and the propaganda of luxury, have you a nice simple answer? One has worked on certain materials trying to establish bases and axes of reference. In writing so as to be understood, there is always the problem of rectification without giving up what is correct. There is the struggle not to sign on the dotted line for the opposition.[13]

This is Pound's most valuable comment on his own work because it directs the reader's attention to the content and context of *The Cantos* and not to such sidetracks as analogies with certain musical or plastic paradigms that the format may or may not display.

The statement also emphasizes an important but somewhat neglected word in the lexicon of Pound's key terms: *struggle*. Life and art are not completed products that repeat ideal forms in some final, static way. They are, rather, processes in which pairs of powerful forces—life and death, knowledge and ignorance, freedom and slavery—struggle for domination. Clearly, such long poems as Homer's and Dante's are remote models, for they package a cosmos in terms of perfected forms with causes, beginnings, ends, tops, and bottoms. Instead of these complete triumphs of poetry embodying a set of ideals shared by an audience, Pound is working with materials that are personal and not completely knowable. One may think here of poets like Wordsworth and Whitman who centered their work on the individual personality rather than on some matrix of religious and philosophical convention. For the form of the struggle, one may think of the great monuments, ambitious and unfinished—*The Canterbury Tales*, *The Faerie Queene*, *Don Juan* —that posed such problems that their poets did not live to complete them. A few sentences in *Guide to Kulchur* hint at Pound's kinship with other such strugglers:

> Boccherini, Op. 8 N.5 (as played by the New Hungarian Four) is an example of culture. Bartok's Fifth Quartet under same conditions (March 5th, 1937, Rapallo) is the record of a personal struggle, possible only to a man born in the 1880s.
>
> It has the defects or disadvantages of my Cantos. It has the defects or disadvantages of Beethoven's music, or of as much of Beethoven's music as I can remember. Or perhaps I shd. qualify that: the defects inherent in a record of struggle.
>
> [*GK*, pp. 134–35]

One conspicuous feature—not necessarily a defect—of such struggles in art is the departure from conventional forms. Bartok's Fifth Quartet, like Beethoven's Fifteenth, has five movements instead of the usual four. Beethoven's Ninth Symphony is a cathedral of innovations: in the fourth movement themes from previous movements are repeated and, in one of the most striking novelties in symphonic music, rejected. The tenor says, "O friends, not these tones"—and this must be one of the earliest examples of a work of art that seems to reject parts of itself. As in "Near Perigord," the artist is faithful to his subject matter to such a degree that the form originally chosen for its expression must ostensibly be discarded. The conventional symphonic shapes perfected by Haydn and Mozart with four independent movements arranged in a limited set of tempi and forms (and with no chorus) would not do. Beethoven lengthened all of the movements beyond normal expectations and in the fourth movement introduced a chorus that explicitly and self-consciously disdains the various orchestral themes that have gone before. The form neither shapes nor contains the matter; the matter breaks the ostensible form and makes a new form, unique and unrepeatable.

"End fact. Try fiction" in "Near Perigord" bears a considerable resemblance to "O friends, not these tones." The shape of *The Cantos* is irregular because the poet, after many trials and experiments, cannot find a symmetrical format for his subject. Untitled, unfinished, released periodically as drafts, *The Cantos* is the record of a poet's largely unsuccessful struggle to locate aesthetic correlatives for his vision of the world. The earliest Cantos, written in rough blank verse, began with an act of homage to Browning's *Sordello*, but Browning's example was rejected and the poem was started in a new way, with a multiple ritual of homage to Homer, Renaissance Latin, and Old English versification. Even these debts are provisional, and by the end of Canto I, it should be obvious to the reader that Pound is not rewriting any previous poem—Homer's, Dante's, or Browning's—in modern dress.

There is a good deal of filial piety in the family of poets; the *Aeneid* pays homage to the *Odyssey*, and Dante in turn makes Virgil his guide to the underworld. But homage is not imitation. The world has changed so much that the perfected patterns of formal comedy that worked for Homer and Dante will not work for Pound. He says in *A B C of Reading*, "I don't recommend anyone ELSE to try to do another *Tristram Shandy*,"[14] and what is now Canto II opens with a farewell to another exemplar: "Hang it all, Robert Browning, / there can be but the one 'Sordello.' "[15]

One subject of *The Cantos* is the serious and sometimes desperate search for a form; and the form in use often seems to be deliberately and significantly a nonform. Canto CXVI sounds like an admission of formal failure:

> *But the beauty is not the madness*
> *Tho' my errors and wrecks lie about me.*
> *And I am not a demigod.*
> *I cannot make it cohere.*

[C, pp. 795–96]

Although perfection of form is not possible, however, the poet reaffirms his belief in coherence and offers his broken poem as a partial testament:

> *i.e. it coheres all right*
> > *even if my notes do not cohere.*
> *Many errors,*
> > *a little rightness,*
> *to excuse his hell*
>
> > *and my paradiso. . . .*
> *To confess wrong without losing rightness:*
> *Charity I have had sometimes,*
> > *I cannot make it flow thru.*
> *A little light, like a rushlight*
> > *to lead back splendour.*

[*C*, p. 797]

It seems necessary, then, to read *The Cantos* as a record—what Pound calls, twice in Canto CXVI, "the palimpsest"—of processes of discovery and bewilderment. One may admire the purity and perfection of form in the *Odyssey* and the *Commedia*, but one realizes that their victory was achieved in contexts (early Greek and medieval Catholic cosmology) no longer generally appropriate. *The Cantos* may appear to be a pitiful failure if considered exclusively in aesthetic terms; but in trying so vigorously to write such a long poem that is true to the complexities, obscurities, and ambiguities of modern experience, Pound displayed exemplary honesty and courage.

I see *The Cantos* as the record of the poet's personal and artistic struggle to resist the killing flood of time. The primary impulses of the shorter poems—to catch the present and unearth the past—continue in *The Cantos* on a grand scale that embraces the whole planet's total of history. Descent and metamorphosis are obviously crucial, for the poetic act involves a visit to the land of the lost dead who are somehow brought back to life. The surface of *The Cantos* presents the image of a modern man struggling with his materials, most of them literary and historical texts that themselves present rhyming figures of men—Odysseus, Malatesta, Confucius, John Adams—heroically struggling to deliver order and beauty out of the chaos of their world.

The context of this multiple record of struggles is a peculiar moral and metaphysical system that is like a religion but not conformable to the doctrines of any known church. It is ultimately this moral peculiarity that, much more than the verbal or formal irregularity, makes the poem difficult. Pound concocted a one-man church with *The Cantos* as both bible and temple. For that reason, the precise ethical value of certain acts and qualities is almost impossible to determine. Pound's "Kung" (who bears about as much relation to the historical Confucius as Pound's "Rihaku" does to the real Li Po) urges civic order in Canto XIII, for example, but he also indulges in a sort of antinomian relativism:

> And Thseng-sie desired to know:
>   "Which had answered correctly?"
> And Kung said, "They have all answered correctly,
> "That is to say, each in his nature."

[C, p. 58]

Again, the sage recommends the practice of paternal love in a way that would, under most systems of civic order, make one an accessory after the fact:

> And they said: "If a man commit murder
>   "Should his father protect him, and hide him?"
> And Kung said:
>   "He should hide him."

[C, p. 59]

In the same moral universe there is room for a complaint against pity because that virtue "spareth so many an evil thing" (C, p. 147). But this attitude becomes the cause of slight regret in Canto LXXVI, where an admission is made:

> J'ai eu pitié des autres
> probablement pas assez, and at moments that suited my
>   own convenience.

[C, p. 460]

And even later, in Canto XCIII, this admission turns into a cry of shame:

> *J'ai eu pitié des autres.*
>> *Pas assez! Pas assez!*
>>>> [C, p. 628]

It is clear from one part of the poem to another that the poet is changing his attitude, but in any one part the reader cannot be sure which elements are good and which evil.

We have already looked at Pound's use of myth, magic, and his own "unofficial mysticism" with regard to *Collected Shorter Poems*.[16] The roots of these beliefs are personal and not institutional; an individual undergoes an experience that seems to transcend his corporeal limits, and in order to tell others about his feelings, he objectifies them as myth. If the personal experience, however mysterious, turns out to be common to many members of a community, then the shared belief and its mythic embodiment may develop into religion. For Pound, the essence of these religious modes of experience remains individual and internal, so that he defines a god as "an eternal state of mind."[17] Again and again he traces the abstract entities of religion and philosophy back to individual states of thought and feeling. "The Renaissance," he says in *The Spirit of Romance*, "is not a time, but a temperament."[18] He also denies the objective existence of hell in time and space, not only for himself but for Dante as well:

There is little doubt that Dante conceived the real Hell, Purgatory, and Paradise as states, and not places. Richard St. Victor had, somewhile before, voiced this belief, and it is, moreover, a part of the esoteric and mystic dogma. For the purposes of art and popular religion it is more convenient to deal with such matters objectively; this also was most natural in an age wherein it was the poetic convention to personify abstractions, thoughts, and the spirits of the eyes and senses, and indeed nearly everything that could be regarded as an object, an essence, or a quality. It is therefore expedient in reading the *Commedia* to regard Dante's descriptions of men's mental states in life, in which they are, after death, compelled to continue: that is to say, men's inner selves stand visibly before the eyes of Dante's intellect, which is guided by a personification of classic learning, mystic theology, and the beneficent powers.[19]

Several years later, in a letter written in early 1932, he says of Cantos XIV and XV: "The hell cantos are specifically LONDON, the state of English mind in 1919 and 1920." In the same letter he admits that his "Sir Zenos Metevsky" is to be identified conditionally with the real Sir Basil Zaharoff: "Metevsky is definitely Zaharoff, so far as the facts could be ascertained at the time—none of them essentially contradicted since. Tho of course he stands for a type and a state of mind; and an error in detail won't invalidate him" (*Ltrs*, p. 239).[20]

In view of this emphasis on states of mind, I think it can be said that the primary impulse of *The Cantos* is mystical. Gods exist for Pound because he has undergone certain experiences and because certain mythic correlatives enable him to harmonize his experiences with those of others. He is practical, and the basis of his mysticism is empirical. He does not achieve an ecstatic union with some abstraction by mouthing a formula and following a dietary and pharmaceutical regimen; he does not report his findings in the rather startling terms of Blake's "memorable fancies" ("The prophets Isaiah and Ezekiel dined with me"). But Pound does register a powerfully felt belief in the existence of the eternal states of mind that he calls gods, and he sympathetically records the testimony of other seers. In Canto XIII he tells of Kung's attack on a pretender:

> And Kung raised his cane against Yuan Jang,
> > Yuan Jang being his elder,
> For Yuan Jang sat by the roadside pretending to
> > be receiving wisdom.
> And Kung said
> > "You old fool, come out of it,
> "Get up and do something useful."

> [*C*, pp. 58–59]

But if the mystical vision has a practicable relation to moral questions, then Pound (at least in *Guide to Kulchur*) seems willing to accept the reality of the vision, however idiosyncratic or novel:

At least two kinds of statement are found in philosophy. Spinoza writes:
The intellectual love of things consists in the understanding of their perfections.

Swedenborg, if you permit him to be called a philosopher, writes: I saw three angels, they had hats on their heads.

Both carry conviction. One may be a bit in the dark as to what constituted Swedenborg's optic impressions, but one does not doubt that he had such impressions.

The standard of conduct among angels in his third heaven furnishes an excellent model for those of us who do not consider that we have entered that district.

[*GK*, pp. 73–74]

If no standard of conduct could be inferred from the behavior of the angels seen and described by Swedenborg, then presumably Pound would dismiss him as an "old fool" of Yuan Jang's category.

The poet's search for the meaning of the present and the past is a syncretic attempt to discover spirits that are timeless, and the struggle takes him into realms of gods and other unseen forces. It also takes him to imaginary times and places: a Cathay where the spirit of Confucianism produces good government or a medieval Europe where Catholic philosophers describe luminous precincts of pure Form. His long study of Cavalcanti (1934) is one of his last full-scale attempts to resuscitate a dead figure from the lost past, and in this remarkable essay he strikes a note of melancholic nostalgia:

We appear to have lost the radiant world where one thought cuts through another with clean edge, a world of moving energies "*mezzo oscuro rade*," "*risplende in sè perpetuale effecto*," magnetisms that take form, that are seen, or that border the visible, the matter of Dante's *paradiso*, the glass under water, the form that seems a form seen in a mirror, these realities perceptible to the sense, interacting, "*a lui si tiri*" untouched by the two maladies, the Hebrew disease, the Hindoo disease, fanaticisms and excess that produce Savonarola, asceticisms that produce fakirs, St. Clement of Alexandria, with his prohibition of bathing by women. . . .

For the modern scientist energy has no borders, it is a shapeless "mass" of force; even his capacity to differentiate it to a degree never dreamed by the ancients has not led him to think of its shape or even its loci. The rose that his magnet makes in the iron filings, does not lead him to think of the force in botanic terms, or wish to visualize that force as floral and extant (*ex stare*).[21]

The struggle recorded in *The Cantos* is incomplete; the fragmentary and obscure form of the poem does not reflect a chaotically disordered mind but rather the continually interrupted effort of a visionary intelligence to arrange the materials of history and immediate experience in an aesthetically acceptable form. The "real poem" in Pound's mind that has cast a fitful shadow called *The Cantos*, one might say, can be grasped only as one grasps the eternal states of mind called gods: through incomplete and obscure evidence. Paradoxically, the irregularity and lack of finish are themselves a part of the significance of the whole work. In a way, such a production is an admission of failure, and labeling something a "draft" or a "fragment" may preclude a degree of criticism that would apply to an ostensibly finished product. All criticism of *The Cantos* is necessarily incomplete, because the work itself was not finished; and to almost any imaginable objection—of obscurity, disorder, malevolence, ignorance—the writer could have answered, "Just wait." But except for the first few Cantos, Pound never revised the earlier drafts in any substantial way; he was publishing a serial fragment, and even if he had lived longer than eighty-seven years, I think it is extremely unlikely that we would have ever seen a finished poem that differs in any meaningful particular from the pieces that are now available. Moreover, I think that is perfectly all right.

As it is, the poem faithfully and vividly records the poet's struggle to achieve order and peace. Since it is such a record, the poem should not be indiscriminately praised for its unity or condemned for its lack of unity. The energy and unity of its impulse are clear, but it is equally clear that that most laudable impulse cannot give a recognizable degree of order to the materials of the modern consciousness as experienced by Pound. A ragbag *The Cantos* may be; but it seems to me that these rags in this bag make up a more respectable aesthetic act of the human will than almost any other work of this century. Pound's position in the poem is a balanced compromise. He avoids the extreme of desensitized materialism as well as the extreme of oblivious mysticism. As we have seen in most of his work, he expresses various forms of belief in states of timelessness that transcend mundane experience, but he habitually grasps these states through concrete processes and insists that the value of any idea—even Swedenborg's account of angelic haberdashery—is a function of its efficiency in action.

In the late 1920s, when most of Pound's literary work was devoted to the third decad of *The Cantos*, he was involved in a critical struggle to reconcile the internal, subjective requirements of composing a record of his consciousness and the external, objective requirements of aesthetic design. We have seen that he concentrates on problems of language in "How to Read" to such an extent that he has little to say about architectonics. [22] Just a few months before "How to Read" was published, he practically dismissed the whole idea of general form in literature. In the *Dial* for November 1928 he offered some remarks on the work of William Carlos Williams that apply to his own poetry as well:

Very well, he does not "conclude"; his work has been "often formless," "incoherent," opaque, obscure, obfuscated, confused, truncated, etc.

I am not going to say: "form" is a non-literary component shoved on to literature by Aristotle or by some non-litteratus who told Aristotle about it. Major form is not a non-literary component. But it can do us no harm to stop an hour or so and consider the number of very important chunks of world-literature in which form, major form, is remarkable mainly for absence. . . .

Art very possibly *ought* to be the supreme achievement, the "accomplished"; but there is the other satisfactory effect, that of a man hurling himself at an indomitable chaos, and yanking and hauling as much of it as possible into some sort of order (or beauty), aware of it both as chaos and as potential. . . .

To come at it another way: There are books that are clever enough, good enough, well enough to fool the people who don't know, or to divert one in hours of fatigue. There are other books—and they may be often less clever, and may often show less accomplishment—which, despite their ineptitude, and lack of accomplishment, or "form," and finish, contain something for the best minds of the time, a time, any time. [23]

I think that if we see *The Cantos* as the record of a dynamic process —a mode of activity and not the imprint of an accomplished act, a graph that traces the typical motions of "a man hurling himself at an indomitable chaos"—then two errors can be avoided. The exoteric critic errs by assuming that *The Cantos* is little but chaos with none of the potential for order realized; the esoteric critic errs by assuming that the poem is not a process but a product in which the chaotic materials are ordered into a beautiful form by the operation of some single unifying principle—allegorical, dramatic, epistemological, political, or personal.

The best summary of the battle between these two critical camps is in Daniel D. Pearlman's study of *The Cantos* called *The Barb of Time*. Pearlman makes it clear that the argument about form is the major dividing line between the two camps, he summarizes the cases on both sides, and he shows how Pound himself contributed to the antagonism by his admirable reluctance to explain his poem clearly. Pearlman then offers his own very interesting hypothesis on the nature of *The Cantos*: that the poem does present a unity and uniformity of progress and that this major form is generated by the interactions between the human spirit and various categories of time. Pearlman has obviously studied *The Cantos* carefully, but there are serious flaws that vitiate *The Barb of Time*. Although Pearlman has assumed a grand three-level development that is parallel to conventional Augustinian, Dantean, and Hegelian schematizations of states of mind, he does not show how this development finally determines the specific order of individual units in *The Cantos*. Canto XIII, a description of Kung and his disciples placidly trading moral maxims, is out of place in an inferno. Pearlman, moreover, stops his analysis with *The Pisan Cantos*; that is, he ignores all of Pound's poetry after 1948, which amounts to three volumes containing some three dozen Cantos. Skipping the last quarter of a work is no way to discover its principle of unity. As Pound once said, "Four sections of a poem written in 12 sections do not constitute the whole poem" (*Ltrs*, p. 230). By misinterpreting certain parts of *The Cantos* and ignoring certain others, Pearlman weakens his overall argument to such a degree that his book has value only for its detailed exegesis of isolated passages.

Such unity as *The Cantos* does present is essentially a question of impulse and struggle. The primary impulse in *The Cantos* is the desire to escape chaos by means of patterns of perception and expression that capture the valuable features of the flowing present and the dead past. The technical imperatives of such a desire are not categorical but hypothetical, so that the poet is free to expand all imaginable "unities"—not only time, place, and action but also language, style, character, attitude, and tempo—until the poem is a complex network for catching time. In Pound's social writings we have seen the operation of a general idea of permanent human values that go into action in ways determined by time, place, and culture. We have seen as well in his criticism a similar dialectic of timeless states whose mode of absolute being enters the stream of conditional becoming at some such concentrated node of art as the image or the persona. *Collected Shorter Poems* offers a set of partially realized states of consciousness in which the mindless flux of time is transcended by fame, magic, art, and love. Behind all of these works there is a figure, "Ezra Pound," constantly struggling (and not always succeeding) in labors to combine invention and convention in a way that preserves enduring orders of value and beauty. He separates the living from the dead without regard to chronology: not everyone in the present is living, not everyone in the past is dead. As we have seen, one central question in his work is summed up in "Coda":

> O my songs,
> Why do you look so eagerly and so curiously
>   into people's faces,
> Will you find your lost dead among them? [24]

"Canto" means "song," and the same question applies to *The Cantos*, one axis of which is the struggle to find the lost dead, in many senses.

Canto I begins and ends with "and" and "so that," conjunctions that do not really conjoin any visible syntactic units; this fragment functions as a microcosmic cross section of the poet's whole effort, for the writing on the page represents not a static product but a dynamic process that begins and ends *in medias res* and also *in medias sententiae*.[25] Such a process is a continuing transfer of energy that is reflected in both the main subject of the Canto (a voyage to the underworld) and its main technique (translation from a mixed Greek and Latin idiom into a combination of Old and Modern English). Moving thus among many times, places, and languages, the poem is unusually sensitive to an uncommonly wide range of data; at the same time its innately unstable structure may prefigure the ultimate collapse of the poem as a coherent work of art.

Throughout the poem, from the abrupt "Lie quiet Divus" in Canto I (*C*, p. 5) and "Hang it all, Robert Browning" in Canto II (*C*, p. 6) all the way to the end of *Thrones*, the reader should be aware of a poet actively *addressing* his materials, so that the translation of words and transfer of themes from idiom to idiom are parts of a process that is taking place on the page. The technique of running translation animates the Malatesta Cantos (VIII–XI):

> *And the King o' Ragona, Alphonse le roy d'Aragon,*
> *   was the next nail in our coffin,*
> *And all you can say is, anyway,*
> *that he Sigismundo called a town council*
> *And Valturio said "as well for a sheep as a lamb"*
> *   and this change-over* (haec traditio)
> *As old bladder said "rem eorum saluovit"*
> *Saved the Florentine state.*

> [*C*, p. 35]

This manner is didactic, but it is also autodidactic, for the poet seems to be trying to teach something to himself as well as to his reader; it is present in Cantos XX, XXII, XXIII, XXV, and in great detail in Canto XLIII:

> *Maister Augustino Chisio equites*
> *anointed of the order of Stephen (pope, holy)*
> *ducatorum? no. ducentorum*

> *a return of 10,000 scudi*
> *in the parish of San Giovanni (Joannis)*
> *To be or not to be tied up with the Pawn Shop*
> *and his successors in the Great Duchy*
> > *guarantee of the income from grazing*
> *up to (illegible) said to mean, no . . .*
> *libris septem, the sum of, summam, scutorum*
> *ten thousand.*

[*C*, pp. 217–18]

The surface of translation is missing in *The Pisan Cantos*, where the incarcerated poet has no library to speak of, but it comes forward again in *Section: Rock-Drill*, especially in Canto XCV, which ends with a translation of part of Book V of the *Odyssey*. Canto XCVI, which opens *Thrones*, continues this translation and also includes notes on the inadequacy of dictionaries: "Wang's middle name not in Mathews" (*C*, p. 653) and a Greek word "which is not in Liddell D. D." (*C*, p. 656). A culmination of the step-by-step technique of translation comes in an examination of Chinese laws in Canto XCIX:

> *To discriminate things*
> > *shih$^{2-5}$ solid*
> *mu^2 a pattern*
> *fa^1 laws*
> *kung^1 public*
> *szu^1 private*
> *great and small.*

[*C*, p. 694]

Drafts & Fragments, which represents the harvest of partial wisdom from the poet's struggle against chaos, contains very little of this sort of active translation.

A great deal of what is in *The Cantos* was originally said by someone other than Ezra Pound. Interludes of reflection and consolidation like *The Pisan Cantos* and *Drafts & Fragments* seem to be largely his own creation, but in much of the work the poet's real job is translation or transcription of the words of others, often re-arranged or fragmented, in an attempt to create patterns of sense out of masses of historical data. (It is important to note that there is much more of formal translation as such in *The Cantos* than in *Cathay* and *Homage to Sextus Propertius*.) *The Cantos* looks more like an anthology, chrestomathy, or palimpsest than a poem in the usual sense, because the poet habitually deals with his materials at second hand, and even more often, at third or fourth hand.

The technical process of translation is paralleled by the thematic process of the metaphoric voyage adumbrated in Canto I. There is a Homeric ship in the first line of Canto I and a Dantean dinghy in the last line of Canto CIX (at the end of *Thrones*); the reader should recall how the poet uses the word *periplum* to indicate a circum-navigation as well as the written log of such a voyage. The *Periplus* of Hanno the Carthaginian is quoted in Canto XL, and Pound's definition of the word is given in Canto LIX:

> *periplum, not as land looks on a map*
> *but as sea bord seen by men sailing.*

> [*C*, p. 324][26]

The restless movement of the later parts of the poem is described and exemplified in a key passage near the end of Canto LXXIV:

> *By no means an orderly Dantescan rising*
> *but as the winds veer*
>
>   *tira libeccio*
> *now Genji at Suma   , tira libeccio*
>   *as the winds veer and the raft is driven*
>   *and the voices   , Tiro, Alcmene*
>   *with you in Europa nec casta Pasiphaë*
>   *Eurus, Apeliota as the winds veer in periplum*
> *Io son la luna." Cunizza*
>   *as the winds veer in periplum.*

> [*C*, p. 443]

The poet's voyage takes him across the "godly sea" of "spiteful Neptune" (*C*, pp. 3, 5), and the evils of history are regularly expressed in terms of the tidal flux of time. In two widely separated passages Pound represents evil as a "dung-flow" (*C*, pp. 64, 614)— an unending process epitomized in "All things are a flowing," the Heracleitean maxim first used by Pound in *Hugh Selwyn Mauberley*.[27] Variations of this formula are found in Cantos LXXIV, LXXX, LXXXIII, XCVI, and CVII.[28] In a letter written in 1936, Pound mentions "the tiny raft that civilization was floating on" (*Ltrs*, p. 279), and in *Guide to Kulchur*, having just quoted Heracleitus' saying, he claims, "During the downshoot of XIXth century forms there remained a species of surface. A sort of immense cardboard raft intact on, as it were, a cataract of stale sewage" (*GK*, pp. 79–82). In *The Pisan Cantos* he speaks of his personal disaster as a time "when the raft broke and the waters went over me" (*C*, p. 513). The variously transfigured ships of Odysseus and Acoetes move through Cantos I and II; the ending of Canto CIX picks up a line from Dante that first appears in Canto VII ("O voi che siete in piccioletta barca"—*C*, p. 26); it is translated in Canto XCIII:

> "*Oh you,*" *as Dante says*
> > "*in the dinghy astern there.*"
>
> [*C*, p. 631]

In the *Commedia*, which is a most systematic *periplum*, the image of the seafarer occurs near the beginning of each main subdivision. In *Inferno* I, Dante says (in the Carlyle-Wicksteed translation):

> *And as he, who with panting breath has escaped from the deep sea to the shore, turns to the dangerous water and gazes:*
> *so my mind, which still was fleeting, turned back to see the pass that no one ever left alive.*

The *Purgatorio* opens:

> *To course o'er better waters now hoists sail the little bark of my wit, leaving behind her a sea so cruel.*

And Canto II of the *Paradiso* begins with the passage thrice quoted by Pound:

O ye who in your little skiff, longing to hear, have
followed on my keel that singeth on its way,
*   turn to revisit your own shores; commit you not to*
the open sea; for perchance, losing me, ye would be
left astray.

The end of Pound's Canto CIX seems to be a warning and a prom-
ise to the reader that the poet will continue his efforts to piece
together a modern vision of paradise, however "spezzato" and
"jagged" (*C*, pp. 438, 620).

The *periplum*, which takes the poet through seventy-one Cantos
concerned with setbacks and achievements in Mediterranean, Chinese, and American history, is interrupted in *The Pisan Cantos* by an
international disaster that turns fitfully into a Boethian vision of
wisdom. The water previously associated with disorder and destruction is metamorphosed in Canto LXXXIII into a shower of
rain that brings peace. Images of rescue from the wrecking flood
of time occur as early as the fragment of Canto LXXII in a letter
of 12 March 1941. The line "The water-bug's mittens show on
the bright rock below him"[29] subsequently appears in Canto
LXXXVII—"As the water-bug casts a flower on stone"—and in
Canto XCI:

The water-bug's mittens
*   petal the rock beneath,*
The natrix glides sapphire into the rock-pool.

[*C*, pp. 574, 616]

The bug and the water snake (*natrix*) are equipped to withstand the
dangers of water, and their survival provokes metaphors of beauty
like "petal" and "sapphire."

At the end of Canto XCI, in another image of rescue, the poet
introduces the figure of Leucothea, who in Book V of the *Odyssey*
saves Odysseus from drowning when his raft is destroyed. She
advises him to abandon the remnants of the raft and to rely for
salvation on her *kredemnon*, an article of clothing translated by
Pound as "bikini" and "veil."[30] His translation of this part of the

Odyssey, as we have seen, forms the link between *Section: Rock-Drill* and *Thrones*. Canto XCV ends:

> *That the wave crashed, whirling the raft, then*
> *Tearing the oar from his hand,*
> > *broke mast and yard-arm*
> *And he was drawn down under wave,*
> > *The wind tossing,*
> *Notus, Boreas,*
> > *as it were thistle-down.*
> *Then Leucothea had pity,*
> > *"mortal once*
> *Who now is a sea-god:*
> > *νόστου*
> *γαίης φαιήκων, . ."*

[C, p. 647]

Canto XCVI, at the beginning of *Thrones*, resumes the account of the rescue:

> *Κρήδεμνον*
> *κρήδεμνον*
> *and the wave concealed her,*
> > *dark mass of great water.*

[C, p. 651]

Alongside the images of the water-bug and the *kredemnon*, the poet sets fragmented passages concerned with the destruction of the Spanish Armada and a graceful hieroglyph that shows the floating barge of Pound's syncretic goddess of wisdom, "Ra-Set." Homer's epithet for Leucothea is quoted again in Canto CX ("KALLIAS-TRAGALOS," *C*, p. 780) among other figures of redemption—

> *From time's wreckage shored,*
> > *these fragments shored against ruin*

[C, p. 781]

—an allusion to Canto VIII and *The Waste Land.*

Time's wreckage is held off by various means—ships, rafts, barges, magic wimples—that all symbolize the poet's struggle to seize the present and revisit the past, an effort that pervades *The Cantos* in the forms of memory and the measurement of physical time. Partially effaced historical records and the uncertainties of the individual human memory, in fact, account for much of the incompleteness of *The Cantos*. The poet must speak of "the most renowned Johnny something or other de Binis" and "Donna Orsola of wherever" (*C*, pp. 213, 219). An event takes place "in a garden at Ubberton, Gubberton, or mebbe it was some / other damned suburb," and a remark is attributed to "Mr. Rothschild, hell knows which Roth-schild / 1861, '64 or there sometime" (*C*, pp. 232–33). In parts of *The Pisan Cantos*, in which the poet must rely on his agitated memory with no substantial assistance from documents, "whatever" becomes a refrain of uncertainty and impatience:

> *the queen stitched King Carolus' shirts or whatever*
> *while Erigena put greek tags in his excellent verses. . .*
> > *and you might find a bit of enamel*
> > *a bit of true blue enamel*
> > > *on a metal pyx or whatever*
> *omnia, quae sunt, lumina sunt, or whatever . . .*
> > > *Le Paradis n'est pas artificiel*
> *and Uncle William dawdling around Notre Dame*
> *in search of whatever.*

[C, p. 528]

On the following page one finds "the grass on the roof of St What's his name" and, a little later, a sketch of Yeats "at Stone Cottage in Sussex by the waste moor / (or whatever)" (*C*, pp. 529, 534). And in a memorable coinage Pound gives "this day October the whateverth" as the dateline of part of Canto LXXXIV (*C*, p. 537).

To work against such decay of record and memory, Pound seems to be preoccupied with calendars and clocks that help him at least fix the time of some occurrence. Documents are dated in many ways: "terra 1537, carta 136" (*C*, p. 120) and

> *Year 6962 of the world*
> *18th. April, in Constantinople.*

[C, p. 125]

Revolutions rechristen months and cities, as the poet notes: "Brumaire, Fructidor, Petrograd" (*C*, p. 131). Canto XLI, adopting the Italian fascist calendar, dates itself "XI of our era" (*C*, p. 202); *The Pisan Cantos*, set in "the 23rd year of the effort" (*C*, p. 430) is probably the last document of any consequence to measure years in this way. Canto XLIII mentions the "Stile senese or the year beginning in March" (*C*, p. 222), and the poet takes the time to say that Emperor Wu Wang "dated his year from the winter solstice" (*C*, p. 266). John Adams's birth is elaborately documented in Canto LXII: "Born 1735; 19th Oct. old style; 30th new style" (*C*, p. 341), as a reminder that Adams's birth preceded Pound's by 150 years to the day. An interest in the orientation of clocks appears in Canto XLIII:

> *Saturday fourth day of March*
> *at? VIth (hour? after sunrise or whatever)*

[*C*, p. 215]

and again in Canto XCVI, which cites a Byzantine law regarding taverns, which on the Lord's day are

> *not to open before 2 o'clock*
> *by whatever 2 that was reckoned.*

[*C*, p. 661]

The poet of *The Pisan Cantos*, removed from most of his documentary sources and nearly all of the amenities of civilization, turns to affectionate observation of the plant and animal life in his immediate vicinity; some of the finest descriptive writing in these poems comes in passages that, essentially unlike anything in the first seventy-one Cantos, deal with spiders, wasps, grasshoppers, birds, cats, and blades of grass. In the same way, with no clock or calendar to organize the time, the poet must rely only on the cycles of the sun, moon, and stars:

> *The shadow of the tent's peak treads on its corner peg*
> *marking the hour*

[*C*, p. 483]

>   *Till finally the moon rose like a blue p. c.*
> *of Bingen on the Rhine*
> *   round as Perkeo's tub*
> *then glaring Eos stared the moon in the face*

[C, p. 499]

>   *the moon's arse been chewed off by this time*

[C, p. 500]

> *With clouds over Taishan-Chocorua*
> *   when the blackberry ripens*
> *and now the new moon faces Taishan*
> *one must count by the dawn star*

[C, p. 530]

> *A fat moon rises lop-sided over the mountain*
> *The eyes, this time my world,*
> *   But pass and look* from *mine*
> *   between my lids*
> *   sea, sky, and pool*
> *   alternate*
> *   pool, sky, sea,*
>
> *morning moon against sunrise*
> *like a bit of the best antient greek coinage.*

[C, p. 535]

Near the end of *The Pisan Cantos*, the personified moon is apostrophized by the poet who has practically no other image of beauty, no other calendar, and no other timepiece:

> *Under white clouds, cielo di Pisa*
> *out of all this beauty something must come,*
>
> *O moon my pin-up,*
> *   chronometer.*

[C, p. 539]

The passage of time is unavoidably realized in a complex of images involving flux and mortality, and at moments of great concentration in *The Cantos*, time is mentioned by name. The poet's inquiry into the nature of time and evil comes to rest at one point on an equation: "Time is the evil. Evil" (*C*, p. 147)—a line that introduces a retelling of an episode from Camoëns's *Os Lusiadas* that Pound praised in *The Spirit of Romance*. The story, a gruesome account of the gross bodily resurrection of one of the "lost dead" who populate *The Cantos*, was summarized in the earlier book: "In brief: Constança, wife of Pedro, heir to the throne of Portugal, died in 1345. He then married in secret one of her maids of honor, Ignez da Castro, a Castilian of the highest rank. Her position was the cause of jealousy, and of conspiracy; she was stabbed in the act of begging clemency from the then reigning Alfonso IV. When Pedro succeeded to the throne, he had her body exhumed, and the court did homage, the grandees of Portugal passing before the double throne of the dead queen and her king, and kissing that hand which had been hers."[31] Here the eyes of a dead lady are made to speak, not by a work of art, but by a grotesque political act of homage, and in Canto XXX the episode concentrates the themes of the evil of time and the interactions between the living and the dead:

> *Time is the evil. Evil.*
>> *A day, and a day*
> *Walked the young Pedro baffled,*
>> *a day, and a day*
> *After Ignez was murdered.*
> *Came the Lords in Lisboa*
>> *a day, and a day*
> *In homage. Seated there*
>> *dead eyes,*
> *Dead hair under the crown,*
> *The King still young there beside her.*

[*C*, pp. 147–48][32]

The presence of this royal corpse is a reminder of Pound's mingling of past and present, living and dead, in a parable (or travesty) of resurrection that indicates the powers of art and love against mortality. He said once of *Homage to Sextus Propertius*, "My job was to bring a dead man to life, to present a living figure" (*Ltrs*, p. 149); and he considered Odysseus "the live man among duds."[33] Baffled by the evil of time, men are forced into visits to one underworld or another; Canto VII includes a ghostly vision of the living dead:

> *And all that day, another day:*
> > *Thin husks I had known as men,*
> *Dry casques of departed locusts*
> > *speaking a shell of speech . . .*
> *Propped between chairs and table . . .*
> *Words like the locust-shells, moved by no inner being;*
> > *A dryness calling for death.*

[C, p. 26]

A similar scene is suggested at the end of Canto XLV:

> *Corpses are set to banquet*
> *at behest of usura.*

[C, p. 230]

The figure of Tiresias, "who even dead, yet hath his mind entire" (*C*, p. 236), is a reversal of the theme of the dead among the living; and in two anecdotes the poet provides yet another variation:

> *And old Pills who tried to get him into a front*
> > *rank action*
> *In order to drive the rear guard at his buttocks,*
> *Old Pills listed among the murdered, although he*
> *Came out of jail living later.*

[C, p. 46]

> *And Metevsky died and was buried,* i.e. *officially,*
> *And sat in the Yeiner Kafé watching the funeral.*

[C, p. 81]

At the end of Canto XXXIV, time and space, considered as potential military disadvantages, are combined in a figure of mud:

> *French army 500 thousand, the Russian 300 thousand,*
> *But counting on space and time.*
> *"The fifth element: mud." said Napoleon.*
>
> > [C, pp. 165–66]

This ironic quintessence recurs in Canto LI next to a vision of divine light:

> *Shines*
> *in the mind of heaven   God*
> *who made it*
> *more than the sun*
> *in our eye.*
> *Fifth element; mud; said Napoleon.*
>
> > [C, p. 250]

This juxtaposition of light and mud is an elemental paradigm of the struggle of *The Cantos* to escape the limits of time and space. At the end of this key Canto, the poet says, "Time was of the League of Cambrai" (*C*, p. 252). This league was only temporarily successful, so that the line may mean that time, as a military ally, is ultimately powerless. The passage is extremely condensed, and it is difficult to square this interpretation with the shrewd, successful use of time (and space) by the Russians in Canto XXXIV, but from the general context it is clear that the poet means to deny any awesome authority to the figure of Time.

We have seen how the poet pays an unusual amount of attention to calendars and clocks. Quotations from Hesiod's *Works and Days* and an ancient Chinese almanac, the *Li Ki*, in Cantos XLVII and LII point to a less mechanical observation of times and seasons as one way of being in harmony with nature. This theme is summarized in the biblical inscription on the tomb of Isotta degli Atti in Sigismundo Malatesta's Tempio: "Tempus loquendi, tempus tacendi." Observance of the seasons of things, ancient and modern, is given a humorous twist at the beginning of Canto XXXI:

> *Tempus loquendi,*
> *Tempus tacendi.*

> Said Mr. Jefferson: It wd. have given us
>> time.
> "modern dress for your statue....."

[C, p. 153]³⁴

The bewitching influence of Circe in Canto XXXIX causes a confusion of seasons:

> Spring overborne into summer
>> late spring in leafy autumn.

[C, p. 193]

Such disturbance of nature is echoed in parts of the Chinese Cantos that concern periods of political unrest:

> Snow fell in mid summer
>> Apricots were in December
> . . . .
> Rain of blood fell in Y-yang
>> pear trees fruited in winter.

[C, pp. 274, 277]

Against these disturbances the poet urges observance of proper seasons, as in the line "War, letters, to each a time" in Canto LIV (C, p. 285) or in this passage from Canto LXXI:

> they wd/ have united with England and France
> to elucidate the meaning of words at that time
>> and then determine intentions.

[C, p. 413]

Seeing the poet in Canto LXXIV reduced to reading a magazine called *Time* to keep up with its obituaries (C, p. 434), the reader may recall a line from Canto XLVII, "Thus was it in time" (C, p. 237), and several other explicit references to memory, time, and the times:

> el triste pensier si volge
>> ad Ussel. A Ventadour
>>> va il consire, el tempo rivolge

[C, p. 428]

> Huddy going out and taller than anyone present
>   où sont les heurs of that year
>
> [C, p. 433]

> the huntress in broken plaster keeps watch no longer
> tempora, tempora and as to mores
>
> by Babylonian wall (memorat Cheever)
>   out of his bas relief, for that line
> we recall him
>   and who's dead, and who isn't
>   and will the world ever take up its course again?
>
> [C, p. 453]

The memory of the poet in the Pisan camp travels in an agitated *periplum* around his own past experiences and present circumstances; at one climactic point in Canto LXXX, his mind moves from the immediate present further and further into the past—through the music of the American Civil War and the poetry of Horace and Homer—until, in two Greek negatives, it comes to rest for a moment at a point where self and time seem to undergo annihilation:

> "mi-hine eyes hev"
>   well yes they have
> seen a good deal of it
>   there is a good deal to be seen
> fairly tough and unblastable
>   and the hymn...
> well in contrast to the god-damned crooning
>   put me down for temporis acti
> ΟΎ ΤΙΣ
> ἄχρονος
> now there are no more days
> οὔ τις
> ἄχρονος
>
> [C, pp. 498–99]

The intermittent development of the themes of time in *The Cantos* rises from the evil flux of mortal events to visions of orderly recurrence and divine permanence. This pattern comes forward in the pairing of the chaos of war, commerce, and ignorance in Canto XXXV with the perfection of love and memory in Canto XXXVI. The prosaic muddle of "Mitteleuropa" in Canto XXXV is accompanied by a decay of attention and memory:

> *"Comment! Vous êtes tombé si bas?"*
>> *replied General Franchet de Whatshisname*
> *on the part of the french royalist party, showing thus*
> *the use of ideals to a jewish Hungarian baron*
> *with a library (naturally with a library)*
> *and a fine collection of paintings. "We find the land*
>> *overbrained."*
> *said the bojars or whatever the old savages call it.*
>
> [C, p. 174]

In the next Canto (largely an attempt to translate Cavalcanti's "Donna mi priegha"), precisely antithetical qualities are displayed:

> *A lady asks me*
>> *I speak in season*
> *She seeks reason for an affect, wild often*
> *That is so proud he hath Love for a name . . .*
> *Where memory liveth*
>> *it takes its state*
> *Formed like a diafan of light on shade.*
>
> [C, p. 177]

Such serenity and clarity distinguish the poetry of those parts of *The Cantos* that escape from the turmoil of passing time into the realm of ideals "now in the mind indestructible" (C, p. 430), values made permanent by the power of love:

> *What thou lovest well remains,*
>> *the rest is dross*
> *What thou lov'st well shall not be reft from thee*
> *What thou lov'st well is thy true heritage.*
>
> [C, pp. 520–21]

In the later Cantos, indeed, it is timeless love that makes all else possible: "Amo ergo sum, and in just that proportion" (*C*, p. 493).[35] Canto XC ends, "UBI AMOR IBI OCULUS EST" (*C*, p. 609).

Throughout *The Cantos*, as in "Heather" and "Cantus Planus," experiences of intense emotion and illumination are registered as triumphs of love and memory over time and also as moments of mystical union with eternal values. One of the gods in Canto CVI, for example, exists "not in memory, / in eternity" (*C*, p. 752), and in Canto XCV time ceases to exist as a sequence and becomes, instead, "ubique":

> *Deus est anima mundi,*
> > *animal optimum*
> > > *et sempiternum.*
> *Tempus est ubique,*
> > > *non motus*
> > > > *in vesperibus orbis.*
> *Expergesci thalamis, gravat serpella nimbus*
> *Mist weighs down the wild thyme plants.*

[*C*, p. 643]

Then in a somewhat later passage a quotation from Saint Anselm removes the religious experience from the time-space realm entirely:

> *"non spatio, sed sapientia"*
> > *not in space but in knowing.*

[*C*, p. 746]

Some readers are disappointed that what should be the "paradise" of Pound's poem is cluttered with scraps from a dozen foreign languages and a great tissue of unpleasant historical detail. It should be clear, however, that the poet's experience of paradise is only sporadic, and the poem faithfully reflects this feature of his thought, just as it reflects the extreme syncretism of his equivalent for religious belief. During his last thirty-five years he struggled to achieve a poetic fusion of his mystical experiences and his political opinions. The intensity and difficulty of this struggle are clearly apparent in *The Cantos*, particularly in those parts of the poem that deal with Chinese and American history; but nowhere, I think, is the depth of his feelings better registered than in a letter he sent to his lawyer, Julien Cornell, from the prison ward of Saint Elizabeths Hospital in 1946:

> *Dungeon*
> *Domenica*
> *end*
> *of Jan,*
>
> *mental torture*
> *constitution a religion*
> *a world lost*
> *grey mist barrier impassible*
>   *ignorance absolute*
>   *anonyme*
> *futility of*
>   *'might have been*
> *coherent areas*
>   *constantly*
>   *invaded*
>   *aiuto*
>   *Pound.*[36]

The equation of constitution and religion is a key, I think, to the poem that Pound wanted *The Cantos* to be: a world epic of positive general culture infusing all human activities with justice and love. In the writings of John Adams that make up much of Cantos LXII–LXXI, the focus is on the labors of the American revolutionaries to establish a just constitution, and Pound's table of contents gives "Plan of Government" (*C*, p. 256) as one of the main topics. He ends this group of Cantos with six lines from "Hymn of Cleanthes, part of Adams' *paideuma*," which he translates: "Glorious, deathless of many names, Zeus aye ruling all things, founder of the inborn qualities of nature, by laws piloting all things" (*C*, p. 256). Later, at the beginning of *The Pisan Cantos*, the details of the "enormous tragedy" of the world are counted off:

> *militarism progressing westward*
> *im Westen nichts neues*
> *and the Constitution in jeopardy*
> *and that state of things not very new either.*

[*C*, p. 426]

The poet states his own fidelities later in the same Canto (LXXIV):

> *I surrender neither the empire nor the temples*
>   *plural*
> *nor the constitution nor yet the city of Dioce*
> *each one in his god's name.*

[*C*, pp. 434–35]

In Canto XCV, the evils of political ignorance and obfuscation are opposed by the rescue of Odysseus:

> *Among all these twerps and Pulitzer sponges*
>   *no voice for the Constitution,*
> *No objection to the historic blackout.*
>   *"My bikini is worth yr/ raft." Said Leucothae* [sic].

[*C*, p. 645]

"God bless the Constitution / and *save* it," Pound says, ". . . and god damn the perverters" (*C*, p. 486). The poet's religious fervor for the Constitution, indeed, consistently provokes him into mild profanity in the defense of its principles; this could be called the "consti-damn-tution" (*C*, p. 418) tmesis-syndrome. He disapproves of Prohibition, for example, and praises Congressman George H. Tinkham:

> *Two with him in the whole house against the constriction of*
>   *Bacchus*
> *moved to repeal that god-damned amendment:*
>   *Number XVIII*
>   *Mr. Tinkham.*

[*C*, p. 481]

Later he attacks Article 1, Section 10 (which denies certain powers to the states) in terms that recall both his outbursts of blasphemy and the "constitution a religion" in the letter to Cornell:

> *"That Virginia be sovreign,"* said Andy Jackson
>   *"never parted with..."*
>   *Oh* GAWD!!! *that tenth section...*
> *"any portion of..."*
>   DAMN IT.
> *George Second encouraged,*
>   *the tariff of 1816 murdered indigo.*
>   *Freemen do not look upward for bounty.*
> *Barley, rice, cotton, tax-free*
>   *with hilaritas.*
> *Letizia, Dante, Canto 18*   *a religion.*
>
>   [*C*, pp. 715–16]

(Part of Canto XVIII of the *Paradiso* deals with the forms and symbols of Roman law.)

But the ideal synthesis of religious, philosophical, and political principles is never realized in *The Cantos*. The poems in *Drafts & Fragments* are notes toward the "paradise" of an unwritten epic. The last line, "To be men not destroyers" (*C*, p. 802), remains as the most important item on an agenda that has yet to be carried out. The shortest fragment, Canto CXX, is an appeal for peace, silence, and forgiveness.

The fragment of Canto CXV is addressed directly to the problems of time and timelessness that we have been considering in all of Pound's work. It contains a brief eulogy on Wyndham Lewis, his old friend and antagonist, along with what seems to be a commentary on Lewis's *Time and Western Man*. The fragment ends with a lament for the present condition of the United States, a homeland where past and present, death and life, are tragically confused. As a conclusion to this study of Pound's handling of ideas of time, I quote all of this fragment:

> *The scientists are in terror*
>   *and the European mind stops*

Wyndham Lewis chose blindness
   rather than have his mind stop.
Night under wind mid garofani,
   the petals almost still
Mozart, Linnaeus, Sulmona,
When one's friends hate each other
   how can there be peace in the world?
Their asperities diverted me in my green time.
A blown husk that is finished
   but the light sings eternal
a pale flare over marshes
   where the salt hay whispers to tide's change
Time, space,
   neither life nor death is the answer.
And of man seeking good,
   doing evil.
In meiner Heimat
   where the dead walked
      and the living were made of cardboard.

[C, p. 794]

APPENDIX: TIME IN
THE STUDY OF
LITERATURE

In most poetry time may function in three manifestations. It is a complex dimension of the physical universe of the represented subject matter; it is a condition of the representing verbal medium; and it can even take the shape of an explicit thematic figure, both in its own form as "time" or "Time" and in the form of myth or metaphor. The action of *The Winter's Tale*, for example, takes up a certain amount of time on the stage and represents a much greater amount of time in the real world; the words of the play are spoken in time; and the chorus is "Time" itself.

The investigation of such phenomena belongs to a branch of study that uses ideas going back at least as far as the Pre-Socratics,[1] but detailed critical work in this field has been done mostly in the past two centuries. The classic examination of time and art remains Lessing's *Laocoön* (1766), a lengthy but incomplete essay that systematizes the connections between time *and* space, considered as necessary qualities of imitated nature, and time *or* space as potential qualities of certain imitating arts. Standards of logic, harmony, and decorum determine the success of the imitation, so that the critic, from Lessing's standpoint, must examine the suitability of the aesthetic matter (such as words or stone) in relation to the aesthetic form (such as action or character).[2]

Lessing extends certain concepts of imitation implicit in Aristotle's *Po-*

127

etics; yet he avoids Castelvetro's practice of translating those concepts into a set of mechanical "unities" based merely on consideration of the physical and mental comfort of the audience.[3] Instead, by means of particular examples that lead to general principles, Lessing describes the various sorts of subject matter best handled by the various sorts of representation. He states his conclusions in the form of aesthetic laws:

> My conclusion is this. If it is true that painting employs in its imitations quite other means or signs than poetry employs, the former—that is to say, figures and colours in space—but the latter articulate sounds in time; as, unquestionably, the signs used must have a definite relation to the thing signified, it follows that signs arranged together side by side can express only subjects which, or the various parts of which, exist thus side by side, whilst signs which succeed each other can express only subjects which, or the various parts of which, succeed each other.
>
> Subjects which, or the various parts of which, exist side by side, may be called *bodies*. Consequently, bodies with their visible properties form the proper subjects of painting.
>
> Subjects which or the various parts of which succeed each other may in general be called *actions*. Consequently, actions form the proper subjects of poetry.[4]

Accordingly, Lessing can explain the failure of quasi-pictorial poetry and quasi-narrative painting by demonstrating how they cannot possibly obey the formal and material imperatives that are inherent in the relation between their chosen objects and their chosen means of imitation. Stated most generally, Lessing's idea proposes that space, an external and objective form of being, is radically different from time, an external and objective form of becoming. This distinction is the basis of almost all subsequent criticism addressed to the problems of time and space in art.

Lessing accepts time and space as axiomatic categories of the physical worlds of nature and art. He does not bother to define them, and he pays no attention to philosophic doctrines that treat time and space as subjective categories of perception and not as eternally necessary conditions of objective existence. The modern critic who tries to apply Lessing's ideas encounters problems of definition with his most important terms, which clearly are not as simple as Lessing's confident handling of them might suggest. The fundamental difficulty (and advantage) is that man understands time in the same way he understands his language and himself: from within. Located indeterminately in a time-space continuum, man can offer definitions of time and space only in a manner that is incomplete, contradictory, or tautologous. "What is time?" Saint Augustine asks. "If no one asks me, I know; if I want to explain it to someone who asks, I do not know."[5] The same predicament faced Charles Lamb when he was writing a letter to a faraway friend: "It is New Year here; that is, it was New Year half a-year back, when I was writing this. Nothing puzzles me more than time and space; and yet nothing puzzles me less, for I never think about them."[6] But perplexing as they may be, such questions must be considered sooner or later in the study of literary works, because such works exist in time while simultaneously representing objects that themselves exist in time.

The necessary fixity of time and space, axiomatic in Lessing's aesthetic, was largely discredited by metaphysicians in his own time. By the nineteenth century, as Jerome Buckley has shown,[7] literature was dominated by patterns of thought that depended on a time-space continuum much less rigid than Lessing's. Temporal change was the controlling matrix for such matched pairs of conceptions as progress and decadence, evolution and entropy, archaism and futurism. Mutability was found to be a fundamental law of nature by scientific researches, first in geology and biology and later in physics and psychology. *Laocoön* can now be seen as one of the last great documents of the period in Western thought when certainty about fixity was possible.

The date of *Laocoön* fits into W. H. McNeill's account of the "Western explosion": "From the perspective of the 1960's, it looks as though the industrial transformations which began in England about two hundred years ago and reached really massive proportions only a little more than a century before our time constituted a mutation in the economic and social life of mankind comparable in magnitude with the Neolithic transition from predation to agriculture and animal husbandry."[8] McNeill traces this "explosion," dating roughly from 1789 to 1917, as it was realized in territorial expansion, industrialism, revolution, and artistic and intellectual aspects of the "developmental-historical point of view."[9] Connections between general modes of thinking and Darwin's specific hypothesis were established early in this century by John Dewey, who pointed out that "the combination of the very words origin and species embodied an intellectual revolt and introduced a new intellectual temper."[10] Ezra Pound, who was born in 1885, began his career at a time when the classical concepts of time and space had so deteriorated that the terms of Lessing's theory needed to be profoundly revised if they were to be of any substantial value.

Conceived, then, *sub specie evolutionis* instead of *sub specie aeternitatis*, time and space surrendered the tidy categorical rigidity that had once allowed Lessing to bypass definitions. Fifty years ago Samuel Alexander wrote, "At the present moment, the special question of the exact relation of Time to Space has been forced into the front, because Time has recently come into its full rights, in science through the mathematical physicists, in philosophy also through Prof. Bergson, who finds in Time conceived as *durée*, in distinction from Time as measured by the clock, the animating principle of the universe." Among the moderns Bergson was, indeed, "the first philosopher to take Time seriously."[11] In his *Essai sur les données immédiates de la conscience* (translated as *Time and Free Will*), Bergson relegates mechanical, static entities of every sort, including even physical time itself, to the realm of "space." Qualities of dynamic vitality are reserved for the uninterrupted continuum of mental states called *durée*, in which past, present, and future interpenetrate in such a way that they cannot be separated. Such a continuous succession of moments is the definition of life itself, and its absence is the same as death, signalized by a separation of moments from each other and by the uniform distribution of time across space in a logical, lifeless pattern.[12]

In aesthetics Bergson applies his idea of *durée* in a variety of forms that stress the importance of verisimilitude to the facts of real durational experience. He says, for example, "Now, if some bold novelist, tearing aside the cleverly woven curtain of our conventional ego, shows us under this appearance of logic a fundamental absurdity, under this juxtaposition of simple states an infinite permeation of a thousand different impressions which have already ceased to exist the instant they are named, we commend him for having known us better than we knew ourselves."[13] Furthermore, according to one of Bergson's most famous ideas, the vital and the mechanical cannot be harmoniously reconciled, and when they are placed together the dissonance causes laughter. "The attitudes, gestures, and movements of the human body are laughable in exact proportion as that body reminds us of a mere machine."[14]

Bergson's ideas were taken up by such younger aestheticians as T. E. Hulme—who accepted Bergson's distinction between extensive mechanical complexities, dealt with by the intellect, and intensive vital complexities, dealt with by the intuition; but Hulme's conclusion, departing from the usual "fluid" interpretation of Bergson's vital intuition in a context of *durée*, is that classic art is "dry and hard."[15] Wyndham Lewis came to much the same conclusion, but in the process he blamed Bergson's mode of thought for every imaginable aesthetic evil.[16] His *Time and Western Man* includes vigorous attacks on a great many contemporary artists—including Chaplin, Stein, Joyce, Pound, and even Anita Loos—all of whom fail because their works embody an unwholesome obsession with subjective time. In Lewis's analysis Bergson's dismissal of the mechanism of the physical world is reflected in false innocence, childishness, archaism, and primitivism. These kinds of aesthetic surrender, according to Lewis, represent thoughts and feelings that are gummily dissolved in the flowing "becoming" medium of time without ever attaining crystallized physical reality in the fixity, clarity, and freshness of space, the medium of ideal being. Pound, a "revolutionary simpleton" and a "man in love with the past," has at least the virtue of being an "authentic primitive"; but Gertrude Stein's pose is that of the "faux naïf." Joyce is condemned for what Lewis considers an uninterrupted immersion in the flux of ordinary time-dominated life.[17]

Although some of Lewis's insights are brilliant, he is too vitriolic and too obscure. By the end of *Time and Western Man*, the reader has begun to feel that Lewis connects "time" with anything he does not like. To put the judgment in developmental-historical terms, his failure lies in his desperate opposition to his own zeitgeist. Roughly contemporaneous with *Time and Western Man*, the novels of Proust, Mann, Joyce, and Faulkner, with their subtle manipulations of temporal and spatial dimensions, made it clear that space-time problems are themselves fit themes for literature. And these creative investigations were accompanied by a resurgence of critical interest in the aesthetics of time.

Edwin Muir's *Structure of the Novel* (1928) followed *Time and Western Man* by a year. There is, however, no evidence that Muir was aware of Lewis's ideas, and it is certain that he avoids Lewis's excesses of disorder and prejudice. Muir divides typical fictional structures into three sorts: novels of action that depend on time for their form, novels of character that depend on space, and "chronicles" that present significant movement in both time and space. Muir does not claim that any novel is purely an account of character without action or action without character; he argues instead that one or the other emphasis prevails and generates the appropriate form in which the changes in the novel take place.[18] More recent studies of fiction[19] add details to Muir's general idea and bring his observations up to date with examples from more recent writers (e.g., Faulkner and Wolfe), but it seems to me that no work matches Muir's rather neglected study, which is comprehensive and at the same time spare and lucid. He argues that in a novel devoted to a revelation of character, changes in time are subordinate, so that the resultant structure can be called "spatial." Space in this sense is not so much a physical term as a metaphor that embodies the formal category that remains when time, as a significant factor in processes of discovery, is subtracted from the aesthetic continuum.[20]

Time is also a problem in the criticism of poetry. In *A Key to Modern British Poetry*, for example, Lawrence Durrell says, "Time is one of the great clues to the modern outlook."[21] Durrell airily summarizes the ideas of modern physicists who have replaced the "old extended time" of earlier scientists with a "new time-space hybrid." Einstein, Durrell says, recombined space and time "into a four-dimensional volume which he called a 'continuum.'" In a physical universe so construed, such concepts as order, causality, location, and certainty suffer an almost unimaginable change. The effect on literature is also enormous. Durrell says, "I do not think it is stretching a point too far to say that the work of Joyce and Proust, the poetry of Eliot and Rilke, is an attempt to present the material of human and supernatural affairs in the form of poetic continuum, where the language no less than the objects observed are impregnated with the new time." Time, in Durrell's analysis, "has become a thick opaque medium, welded to space—no longer the quickly flowing river of the Christian hymns, moving from here to there along a marked series of stages. But an always-present yet always recurring thing."[22]

It is interesting to note that Lewis, Muir, and Durrell all subsequently produced creative works in which they used some of the ideas about time that they first handled as problems of criticism. Lewis's *One-Way Song*[23] is a volume of superior doggerel that repeats many of the ideas in *Time and Western Man*. Muir's long poem, *Variations on a Time Theme*, is of little interest today unless as a painful demonstration of the difficulty of attempting a major theme with inadequate resources. Its opening reads like *The Waste Land* or *Ash Wednesday* slightly, but fatally, out of tune:

> *After the fever this long convalescence,*
> *Chapped blood and growing pains, waiting for life.*
> *Turning away from hope, too dull for speculation.*

Another passage suggests what *Burnt Norton* might be like if Eliot had not been a great poet:

> *If there's no crack or chink, no escape from Time,*
> *No spasm, no murderous knife to rape from Time*
> *The pure and trackless day of liberty;*

> *If there's no power can burst the rock of Time,*
> *No Rescuer from the dungeon stock of Time,*
> *Nothing in earth or heaven to set us free:*
> *Imprisonment's for ever; we're the mock of Time,*
> *While lost and empty lies Eternity.*[24]

Lewis's attack on the perversions of Bergsonism that sanctify an ultimately mindless one-dimensional flux of consciousness receives a measure
of support in a note prefixed to *Balthazar*, the second novel in Durrell's
Alexandria Quartet:

> Modern literature offers us no Unities, so I have turned to science and
> am trying to complete a four-decker novel whose form is based on the
> relativity proposition.
> Three sides of space and one of time constitute the soup-mix recipe of a
> continuum. The four novels follow this pattern.
> The first three parts, however, are to be deployed spatially . . . and are
> not linked in a serial form. They interlap, interweave, in a purely spatial
> relation Time is stayed. The fourth part alone will represent time and be a
> true sequel. . . .
> This is not Proustian or Joycean method—for they illustrate Bergsonian
> "Duration" in my opinion, not "Space-Time."[25]

Durrell's technique has certain similarities to that used in such earlier
works as *The Ring and the Book* and *The Sound and the Fury*. Neither Browning nor Faulkner explicitly related his experiments to scientific developments, but Faulkner did honor Bergson and Proust. "There isn't any
time," he told an interviewer. "In fact I agree pretty much with Bergson's
theory of the fluidity of time. There is only the present moment, in which
I include both the past and the future, and that is eternity. . . . After I
had read *A la Recherche du Temps Perdu* I said 'This is it!'—and I wished I had
written it myself."[26] Comparable arguments against time have been ad-
vanced by several other modern writers, among them Arthur Miller (who
says that the removal of time from a drama facilitates the display of symbolic meanings[27]) and Norman Mailer (one of whose characters is plan-
ning a long work of fiction in which time would be destroyed so that chaos
could be ordered[28]).

Writers and critics may take one side or the other in the space-time
controversy, but the question is, as Henry James said, eternal. The "classic" line of criticism that can be traced from Lessing to Lewis is founded on
a simple ontological assumption that time and space do indeed exist and
that they can be uniformly perceived, distinguished, and imitated. It is

further assumed that time and space are qualitatively different, and it is here, on the problem of value, that Lessing and Lewis disagree. Emphasizing the richness of arts arrayed in a temporal order, Lessing concludes that poetry can better imitate the complex totality of human experience than such static media as painting and sculpture can.[29] Ernest Fenollosa expresses this idea in a single sentence: "One superiority of verbal poetry as an art rests in its getting back to the fundamental reality of *time*." But Fenollosa, examining Chinese poetry in particular, makes claims for it that Lessing would probably find hard to accept. An art form, for Lessing, is largely constrained to exist in either time or space. "Chinese poetry," according to Fenollosa, "has the unique advantage of combining both elements. It speaks at once with the vividness of painting, and with the mobility of sounds. It is, in some sense, more objective than either, more dramatic. In reading Chinese we do not seem to be juggling mental counters, but to be watching *things* work out their own fate."[30] Wyndham Lewis, as we have seen, would agree that space and time are qualitatively different but, having witnessed a "Bergsonian" deterioration of the temporal arts that Lessing could hardly have predicted, would recognize only the power of time to reduce an art form to disorder and not its power to appeal to the imagination.

Durrell, Muir, Mendilow, and other modern critics have attacked the same problems that confronted Lessing, but they have adjusted the original terms of *Laocoön* to reflect radical changes in the ways that physicists and philosophers have come to think about time and space.

Perhaps the most celebrated recent study is Joseph Frank's essay, "Spatial Form in Modern Literature," which first appeared in 1945. Frank suggests that almost all important modern writers have so subverted normal temporal order that the effect is just as if they had somehow turned time into space. Frank salutes Muir briefly in a footnote, and he provides an admirably concise summary of the arguments of Lessing, but he seems to be oblivious to the most valuable implications of their ideas. He praises Lessing for directing critical attention to the physical nature of aesthetic form but arrives at a conclusion—that "spatial" form is superior to "temporal" form—exactly antithetical to Lessing's. Durrell realizes that some modern writers handle time-space as a continuum, and Pound himself suggests this point more than once. But Frank, even after quoting Pound's claim about "freedom from time limits and space limits," insists that modern novels and poems arrest the flux of time by handling it as space and space only. He says, "Modern literature, exemplified by such writers as

T. S. Eliot, Ezra Pound, Marcel Proust, and James Joyce, is moving in the direction of spatial form. This means that the reader is intended to apprehend their work spatially, in a moment of time, rather than as a sequence." Frank supports his hypothesis by paraphrasing Pound's definition of *image*, but he adds one term, *spatially*, that Pound specifically rejects. An image, he says, "is defined, not as a pictorial reproduction, but as the unification of disparate ideas and emotions into a complex presented spatially in an instant of time. Such a complex is not to proceed discursively, according to the laws of language, but is rather to strike the reader's sensibility with an instantaneous impact."[31]

At this point, ignoring Pound's explicit statement that the liberating effect of an image removes time *as well as space* from the universe of the poem, Frank maintains that modern poets are seeking to "overcome the inherent consecutiveness of language, frustrating the reader's normal expectation of a sequence and forcing him to perceive the elements of the poem as juxtaposed in space rather than unrolling in time." Suggesting that Eliot and Pound write poems in which "syntactical sequence is given up for a structure depending on the perception of relationships between disconnected word-groups," Frank prescribes a peculiar technique for reading such poems:

To be properly understood, these word-groups must be juxtaposed with one another and perceived simultaneously; only when this is done can they be adequately understood; for while they follow one another in time, their meaning does not depend on this temporal relationship. The one difficulty of these poems which no amount of textual exegesis can wholly overcome is the internal conflict between the time-logic of language and the space-logic implicit in the modern conception of the nature of poetry. . . . Since the primary reference of any word-group is to something inside the poem itself, language in modern poetry is really reflexive: the meaning-relationship is completed only by the simultaneous perception in space of word-groups which, when read consecutively in time, have no comprehensible relation to each other.[32]

Time and space, logic and language, needless to say, are difficult concepts to manage, and Frank should be granted a measure of latitude in the handling of them. But his idea of the way in which modern poetry should be read seems to me simply wrong. It is hard to believe that he has ever really looked at the evidence. Conceivably, a most superficial examination of *The Waste Land* could persuade an immature reader that its word groups "have no comprehensible relation to each other," but now that the poem has been available for more than fifty years, the relations among the word groups as they unroll in time seems to grow richer with each reading. Even if some of the connections do not follow a simple external temporal logic, it does no good to try to read the poem as something spatial. The reader and the poem exist in time, and all of the elements in the process of experiencing the poem interact in both space and time, or in a space-time continuum. For the reader to attempt to penetrate certain difficulties by simply ignoring one very important dimension of the continuum is to surrender an indispensable part of the aesthetic experience and, briefly, to miss the point.

Visual and auditory "worlds" can, of course, be distinguished from one another, and this separation makes possible aesthetic speculations that otherwise would become unmanageably complex. Lewis and Frank in very different ways prefer the visual, spatial qualities in art. Lessing, on the other hand, valued temporal qualities as an aesthetic medium for reasons that seem to be shared by George Santayana:

The human ear discriminates sounds with ease; what it hears is so diversified that its elements can be massed without being confused, or can form a sequence having a character of its own, to be appreciated and remembered. The eye too has a field in which clear distinctions and relations appear, and for that reason is an organ favourable to intelligence; but what gives music its superior emotional power is its rhythmic advance. Time is a medium which appeals more than space to emotion. Since life itself is a flux, and thought an operation, there is naturally something immediate and breathless about whatever flows and expands. The visible world offers itself to our regard with a certain lazy indifference. "Peruse me," it seems to say, "if you will. I am here; and even if you pass me by now and later find it to your advantage to resurvey me, I may still be here." The world of sounds speaks a more urgent language.[33]

But surely, precisely because life *is* a flux, it is not enough simply to say that the world of the ear is superior as an aesthetic medium to the world of the eye. Even Lessing recognizes that the border between temporal art and spatial art cannot be precisely drawn. He says, "Just as in the one case, with the painter, the two distinct moments touch each other so closely and immediately that they may without offence count as but one, so also in the other case, with the poet, the several strokes for the different parts and properties in space succeed each other so quickly, in such a crowded moment, that we can believe we hear all of them at once."[34] Painting and sculpture do not represent an absolutely static object with all the time removed, and poetry and music do not represent an absolutely dynamic object with all the space removed.

Poetry, especially, partakes of both temporal and spatial orders of existence and of a transcendent imaginative order as well. What Fenollosa claimed for Chinese verse[35] has been extended by Pound to apply to all poetry that is "charged with meaning." Poetry transmits its meaning by appeals to eye, ear, and imagination all at once. The reduction of any single appeal to a unilateral effect leads only to the arrangement of trivial syllables in "concrete" visual formats or in insubstantial jingles. Words do play a part in such predominantly nonverbal creations as posters and songs, but there the full range of possibilities for poetic meaning is subordinated to the much more restricted meaning they can deliver simply by being shapes or sounds. Poetry is not a time art or a space art; it is a complex process that takes place (and takes time, as well) in a rich continuum of physical and psychological dimensions.

Among modern studies of these problems, the most comprehensive is Hans Meyerhoff's *Time and Literature*. Meyerhoff brilliantly locates and analyzes the chief properties of time both as an object of representation and as a condition of expression. He traces the history of temporal presuppositions since the Renaissance and displays the complex system of literal and symbolic linkages between physical time and its psychological counterpart. According to Meyerhoff, the modern temper is so dominated by awareness of changeful time that an individual's consciousness of self and time suffers a breakdown. This disintegration is reflected by works of art and, by being expressed, is to a degree controlled and even corrected. Rigid categories of character and plot are superseded by fluid aesthetic designs that concentrate on consciousness and time, both realized as "streams."[36] Interested chiefly in fiction and philosophy, Meyerhoff discusses few poets —and Pound not at all—but his observations are so useful in general that they can be applied without distortion to poetry. (Needless to say, my handling of Meyerhoff's ideas is nothing like what he himself would conclude in attacking the same questions, but I am pleased nonetheless to acknowledge my debt to his work.)

Recently, C. A. Patrides has edited *Aspects of Time*—containing various critics' essays on time in general and time and modern literature in particular, along with a 562-item bibliography. Even so, it remains surprising that so little study has been devoted to the problems of time in literature and that so little of what has been done concerns poetry. Materials for study are abundant, for in the work of several modern poets—Yeats, Eliot, Stevens, and Hart Crane as well as Pound—time functions as a major thematic and structural principle. In his *Tape for the Turn of the Year*—the finest meditation on time and poetry since *Four Quartets* and *The Pisan Cantos*—A. R. Ammons says:

> in art, we do not run
> to keep up with random
> moments, we select
> & create
> the moment
> occurring forever:
> timelessness held
> at the peak of time

—a reminder that the most practical emblem of modern poetry may be at the end of Dylan Thomas's "Fern Hill":

> And nothing I cared, at my sky blue trades, that time allows
> In all his tuneful turning so few and such morning songs
>   Before the children green and golden
>   Follow him out of grace,
> Nothing I cared, in the lamb white days, that time would take me
> Up to the swallow thronged loft by the shadow of my hand,
>   In the moon that is always rising,
>   Nor that riding to sleep
>   I should hear him fly with the high fields
> And wake to the farm forever fled from the childless land.
> Oh as I was young and easy in the mercy of his means,
>   Time held me green and dying
>   Though I sang in my chains like the sea.

NOTES

PREFACE

1. Ezra Pound, "Date Line," in *Literary Essays*, p. 87.
2. Ezra Pound, *Antheil and "The Treatise on Harmony,"* p. 3. See also pp. 30–47 and Ezra Pound, *Guide to Kulchur*, p. 154. Pound consistently calls the dimension of music "time space."
3. Ezra Pound, *A B C of Reading*, pp. 198–99.
4. Ezra Pound, *Jefferson and/or Mussolini*, p. 62.
5. Ezra Pound, "The Renaissance," in *LE*, p. 217*n*.
6. Ezra Pound, "A Few Don'ts," in *LE*, p. 4.
7. Ezra Pound, *The Cantos*, p. 794.
8. Dudley Fitts, "Music Fit for the Odes," p. 286.
9. William Butler Yeats, ed., *Oxford Book of Modern Verse*, p. xxiv.
10. Charles Olson, *Selected Writings*, pp. 81–82. (In this quotation, as in quotations from Pound's own work throughout this study, I have tried to minimize the use of "sic" while preserving the peculiarities of the original text.) In an earlier work Olson says, "I take SPACE to be the central fact to man born in America, from Folsom cave to now." Charles Olson, *Call Me Ishmael* (1947; reprint ed., New York: Grove Press, 1958), p. 11.
11. Eva Hesse, ed., *New Approaches to Ezra Pound*, p. 38.
12. Hesse, ed., *New Approaches*, pp. 156–57.

CHAPTER 1

1. See T. S. Eliot, "Tradition and the Individual Talent," in *Selected Essays*, pp. 13–22. The essay dates from 1919.

2. Ezra Pound, *Guide to Kulchur*, p. 194.

3. T. S. Eliot, *Four Quartets*, p. 35. This line from "Little Gidding" echoes Mallarmé's "Le tombeau d'Edgar Poe."

4. Ezra Pound, *Letters, 1907–1941*, p. 333.

5. Ezra Pound, *The Spirit of Romance*, p. 8.

6. Ezra Pound, *A Lume Spento and Other Early Poems*, p. 108. The poem originally appeared in *A Quinzaine for This Yule* (1908).

7. Information of this sort can be found in Donald Gallup, *A Bibliography of Ezra Pound*, an indispensable work.

8. Ezra Pound, *Jefferson and/or Mussolini*, p. 19.

9. Ibid., p. 118. *Hysteron proteron*—literally "latter former"—is a rhetorical term that refers to the state of affairs when some natural or rational order is reversed.

10. See Ezra Pound, *A B C of Reading*, p. 81.

11. Wyndham Lewis, *One-Way Song*, p. 19; Wyndham Lewis, *Time and Western Man*, p. 87.

12. Lewis, *Time and Western Man*, p. 87.

13. Richard Ellmann, "Ez and Old Billyum," in *Eminent Domain*, pp. 74–77.

14. Leo Marx, ed., *The Americanness of Walt Whitman* (Boston: D. C. Heath and Co., 1960).

15. Incorporated in Herbert Bergman, "Ezra Pound and Walt Whitman," p. 59.

16. Ibid.

17. Ibid., p. 60.

18. Ibid. Pound's testament, with the spelling normalized, is included in Roy Harvey Pearce, ed., *Whitman: A Collection of Critical Essays*. Pearce suggests two highly improbable interpretations of *maramis*. I think it is a slip of the pen; the intended word is probably *maramus* (a wasting away), which Pound uses often. See, e.g., Ezra Pound, "The Serious Artist," in *Literary Essays*, p. 56.

19. Ezra Pound, *Collected Shorter Poems*, p. 98. The poem, in slightly different form, was first published in *Poetry* in April 1913.

20. Ezra Pound, *Patria Mia*. A preface by the publisher, Ralph Fletcher Seymour, explains that the manuscript was lost and not found until thirty-seven years later. Even if the lost manuscript was a unique copy, Pound could have rewritten the book easily, for most of its contents had appeared in *New Age* in 1912 and 1913 as two series of articles called "Patria Mia" and "America: Chances and Remedies." It is odd that he let the matter drop when the manuscript disappeared.

21. Pound, *LE*, p. 225.

22. Pound points out the practical advantages of his palette: "No one wants the native American artist to be *au courant* with the literary affairs of Paris and London in order that he may make imitations of Paris and London models, but precisely in order that he shall not waste his lifetime making unconscious, or semi-conscious, imitations of French and English models thirty or forty or an hundred years old" (Pound, *LE*, p. 214). "The Renaissance" was published between February and May 1915; in November 1913 he had written to Harriet Monroe, "All I want is that the 'American artist' presuming that he exist shall use not merely London, but Paris, London, Prague or wherever, as a pace-maker. And that he cease to call him

champion for having done 100 yds. in 14 seconds merely because there's no one around to beat him (world's record being presumably 9 85/100)" (Pound, *Ltrs*, p. 25).

23. The reference may be to Havelock Ellis (see Pound, *Ltrs*, p. 133) or to the American author of boys' stories, Edward Sylvester Ellis, who died in 1916.

24. Available in Edmund Wilson, ed., *The Shock of Recognition*, pp. 854–65.

25. I adopt a term applied to Parnell by Yeats in *The Trembling of the Veil* (1922). Yeats uses a similar argument in *The Death of Synge: Extracts from a Diary Kept in 1909*: "When a country produces a man of genius he never is what it wants or believes it wants; he is always unlike its idea of itself. In the eighteenth century Scotland believed itself religious, moral and gloomy, and its national poet Burns came not to speak of these things but to speak of lust and drink and drunken gaiety." William Butler Yeats, *Autobiography*, pp. 132, 352.

26. This praise occurs in "The Renaissance" in a version of an anecdote first recounted in Pound, *Patria Mia*, p. 33. James is not named in either place, but other evidence (e.g., Pound, *Ltrs*, p. 341) makes it clear that Pound has James in mind.

27. William Carlos Williams, *Kora in Hell*, in *Selected Essays*, p. 24.

28. Mouquin, a restaurant in New York, is mentioned again in *The Pisan Cantos* where, as in the letters to Williams, Pound finds himself again in a postwar setting of doubt and disappointment. Ezra Pound, *The Cantos*, pp. 433, 447, 453. (In the quotation from the letter, as throughout this study, I use unspaced periods to indicate an ellipsis in the original text.)

29. Remy de Gourmont, *Querelles de Belgique*, quoted in Pound, *LE*, p. 348.

30. Remy de Gourmont, *Livres des Masques*, quoted in Pound, *LE*, p. 349.

31. Ezra Pound, " 'Dubliners' and Mr. James Joyce," in *LE*, p. 41.

32. Walt Whitman, "By Blue Ontario's Shore," part 6.

33. Presumably "post scriptum Ulixis." Ezra Pound, "The Little Review Calendar," *Little Review* 8 (Spring 1922): 2, 40. See Forrest Read, ed., *Pound/Joyce*, pp. 192–93.

34. Reprinted in Read, ed., *Pound/Joyce*, p. 201.

35. See ibid., pp. 36–40.

36. Further details on the project are in Ernest Hemingway, "Ezra Pound and His Bel Esprit," in *A Moveable Feast*, pp. 95–101; Donald Gallup, "T. S. Eliot and Ezra Pound," pp. 56–57; and Noel Stock, *The Life of Ezra Pound*, pp. 244–45.

37. Ezra Pound, "Le Prix Nobel," in Read, ed., *Pound/Joyce*, p. 219; originally published in *Der Querschnitt*, 4 (Spring 1924): 41–44.

38. In Read, ed., *Pound/Joyce*, p. 176.

39. Ernest Hemingway, "Homage to Ezra," in Peter Russell, ed., *An Examination of Ezra Pound*, p. 75.

40. Read construes the articles that Pound published in the *New Age* during 1919 as the signal that Pound's thought had moved in a new direction, toward politics and economics. See Read, ed., *Pound/Joyce*, pp. 150–51.

CHAPTER 2

1. Ezra Pound, *Literary Essays*, p. 83.

2. Ezra Pound, *The Cantos*, pp. 242, 257, 280.

3. Ezra Pound, *Jefferson and/or Mussolini*, p. iv.

4. Ezra Pound, *Patria Mia*, p. 69.

5. Ezra Pound, *The Spirit of Romance*, pp. 92–93.

6. See above, p. 26.

7. For a partial exoneration of Pound, see John R. Harrison, *The Reactionaries*, pp. 111–42.

8. Pound, *LE*, p. 77.

9. Glyn Daniel, *The Idea of Prehistory*, pp. 82–83.

10. E. E. Cummings, Poem 22, *W (ViVa)*, in *Complete Poems: 1913–1962*, p. 331.

11. Pound, *PM*, pp. 79–80.

12. *Cassell's German and English Dictionary*, 9th ed., p. 281.

13. *OED, Supplement and Bibliography*, s.v. "Kultur."

14. In Forrest Read, ed., *Pound/Joyce*, p. 40.

15. Ezra Pound, *Letters, 1907–1941*, p. 86. In 1931 Pound gave his evaluation of Marianne Moore in a letter to Harriet Monroe: "Kulchuh—more than enough" (Pound, *Ltrs*, p. 235).

16. Ezra Pound, "Henry James," in *LE*, p. 298.

17. Quoted in Joseph Hone, *W. B. Yeats*, p. 433; also in Guy Davenport, "Pound and Frobenius," in *Motive and Method in The Cantos of Ezra Pound*, ed. Lewis Leary, p. 35. Noel Stock says of Pound, "I have not been able to discover when first he began reading Frobenius, but he had correspondence with a Viennese bookshop in February 1930 about buying the seven-volume *Erlebte Erdteile* and the separately published *Paideuma*." Noel Stock, *Reading the Cantos*, p. 30.

18. The quotation is from Laurence Binyon's *The Flight of the Dragon*, which Pound praised in the third of the "Chronicles from *Blast*," in *Pavannes and Divagations*, p. 149; originally published in *Blast* 2 (July 1915): 85–86.

19. Leo Frobenius, *Paideuma*, 3rd ed., p. 39.

20. See ibid., pp. 55–56.

21. Ibid., p. 352.

22. George Eliot, *Middlemarch*, book 1, chapter 3.

23. Susanne K. Langer, *Philosophy in a New Key*, pp. 37–38. The quotations are from *The Childhood of Man* (London, 1909), a translation of Frobenius' *Aus den Flegeljahren der Menschheit* (1901).

24. Davenport, "Pound and Frobenius," p. 45.

25. Ibid.

26. Frobenius, though an increasingly objective student of race and culture, worked willingly under the Nazi regime, which was very congenial to research on *Kultur*. Glyn Daniel has pointed out that "in 1939 courses in prehistoric archeology were given in no less than twenty-five German universities, and archeological research was lavishly supported by the Nazi State" (Daniel, *Prehistory*, p. 120). Curiously, there has been a resurgence of interest in Frobenius among such adherents of "Négritude" as Léopold Sédar Senghor. See his foreword in *Leo Frobenius: An Anthology*, ed. Eike Haberland (Wiesbaden: F. Steiner, 1973).

27. See Pound, *Ltrs*, pp. 288–89.

28. Coleridge calls his own *Biographia Literaria* an "immethodical . . . miscellany" (chapter 4).

29. Donald Davie, *Ezra Pound*, p. 146.

30. Ezra Pound, *Guide to Kulchur*, p. 134. Pound is probably referring to Wyndham Lewis, *Hitler* (1931; rpt. New York: Gordon Press, 1972).

31. This remark appears also in Ezra Pound, Canto L, *The Cantos*, p. 249. Later I shall discuss the connections relating Napoleon, Sigismundo Malatesta ("*against* the current of power"), and Hugh Selwyn Mauberley, who was born "out of date" and whose artistic strivings were "out of key with his time." Ezra Pound, *Collected Shorter Poems*, p. 205.

32. Ezra Pound, *Impact*, p. 247.

33. Ibid., p. 45. This is John Drummond's translation of a revised version of *Carta da visita*, which Pound wrote in Italian.

34. Brooks Adams, *The Law of Civilization and Decay*, pp. viii–ix.

35. Ibid., pp. 354, 360.

36. Ibid., p. 362.

CHAPTER 3

1. In Ezra Pound, *Literary Essays*, p. 4.

2. T. S. Eliot, "The Perfect Critic," in *The Sacred Wood*, p. 11.

3. In Ezra Pound, *Collected Shorter Poems*, p. 119.

4. Ezra Pound, "How I Began," *T. P.'s Weekly*, 6 June 1913, p. 707; reproduced in Noel Stock, ed., *Ezra Pound*, p. 1.

5. Ezra Pound, *Gaudier-Brzeska*, p. 87. The punctuation at the end of the first line of the Metro poem appears as a colon in some places and a semicolon in others. For remarks on the idiosyncratic spacings in the original publication of the poem in *Poetry*, see Hugh Kenner, *The Pound Era*, p. 197.

6. Pound, *Gaudier-Brzeska*, p. 87.

7. Ezra Pound, *The Spirit of Romance*, p. 108.

8. For another examination of "In a Station of the Metro" as an example of Pound's aesthetic in action, see Hugh Witemeyer, *The Poetry of Ezra Pound*, pp. 35–53.

9. Ezra Pound, *Letters, 1907–1941*, p. 131.

10. For a summary of modern developments in the logical representation of ideas, see Max Black, *A Companion to Wittgenstein's Tractatus* (Ithaca: Cornell University Press, 1964), pp. 6–7.

11. Ezra Pound, note to Ernest Fenollosa, "The Chinese Written Character as a Medium for Poetry," ed. Ezra Pound, *Little Review* 6 (September 1919): 62.

12. Fenollosa, 6 (December 1919): 69.

13. See Donald C. Gallup, *A Bibliography of Ezra Pound*, pp. 230–49.

14. William Carlos Williams echoes Pound: "I would say that poetry is language charged with emotion." William Carlos Williams, *Paterson*, p. 261.

15. Pound, *Ltrs*, p. 210.

16. See above, p. 81. The metamorphosis can move from the objective thing in two possible directions: toward the inward subjective world or toward the divine permanent world. At times Pound seems to consider these two modes of metamorphosis—internalization and deification—as essentially a single

phenomenon. His catechism, "Religio, or The Child's Guide to Knowledge," begins: "What is a god? A god is an eternal state of mind." Ezra Pound, *Pavannes and Divisions*, p. 23. I return to this point when I discuss Pound's poetry.

17. "Phanopoeia" and "logopoeia" seem to be Pound's coinages, on analogy with "melopoeia," which is not his invention. In a letter of 17 March 1917 from Pound to Joyce, "Phanopoeia" is mentioned as the possible title of a long poem (clearly *The Cantos*); a suite of poems so titled (not *The Cantos*) appeared in the *Little Review* in November 1918. See Forrest Read, ed., *Pound/Joyce*, p. 102. Pound uses "melopoeia" in the review "Swinburne versus Biographers," *Poetry* 11 (March 1918): 328; in the same month the triad "melopoeia," "imagism," and "logopoeia" appears in Ezra Pound, "A List of Books," *Little Review* 4 (March 1918): 57.

18. Ezra Pound, *Translations*, p. 23. The Introduction to *Cavalcanti Poems* is dated November 1910. The association of word with intellect and rhythm with emotion contains the germ of two later ideas: the "intellectual and emotional complex" in the definition of "image" and the operations of melopoeia and logopoeia. Another early idea that is important here is what Pound called the "method of the Luminous Detail," according to which "certain facts give one a sudden insight into circumjacent conditions." "I Gather the Limbs of Osiris, Part 2," *New Age* 10 (7 December 1911): 130.

19. Pound, *Translations*, pp. 23–24.

20. "Ghosts move about me / Patched with histories"; "And the place is full of spirits"; "Gods float in the azure air." Ezra Pound, "Three Cantos, 1," *Poetry* 10 (June 1917): 114, 116, 118.

21. Pound, "List of Books," p. 57.

22. Pound, "Concava Vallis," part 3 of "Phanopoeia," in *CSP*, p. 188. The poem first appeared, with its title in Greek script, in *Little Review* 5 (November 1918).

23. An attempt to align melopoeia, phanopoeia, and logopoeia with Aristotle's *melos*, *opsis*, and *lexis* is made by Northrop Frye in his *Anatomy of Criticism*, p. 244. This is an engaging and suggestive comparison, but it does not do full justice to the subtleties of Pound's thought. *Melos* and *opsis*—musical accompaniment and scenery (spectacle)—are for Aristotle relatively unimportant formal elements of dramatic poetry, inferior to *lexis* (diction), which, in turn, is subordinate to thought, character, and plot. Pound's theory of the poetic charging of language, concerned almost exclusively with *lexis*, shows the working of words to be somewhat more complicated than the one-to-one relation between words and things assumed by Aristotle. Pound elucidates forms of poetry in which the musical-emotional or visual-visionary impact of language—far from being simply an added attraction to fortify the intellectual content of a given word—is of paramount importance.

24. Ezra Pound, *A B C of Reading*, pp. 73, 193.

25. Verbs are called *Zeitwörter* in German.

26. Ezra Pound, *Jefferson and/or Mussolini*, p. 22. The distinction between noun and verb in terms of time is at least as old as Aristotle, *Poetics* 20. 1457^a 10–19. Evidently, Pound is suggesting that "verbum caro factum est" equals "*verb* made flesh."

27. The essay first appeared in Ezra Pound, *Make It New* (1934), but Pound says it should be dated 1910–31 (Pound, *LE*, p. 149). The crux under discussion is the

phrase "E 'l piacimento / che 'l fa dire amare" (Pound, *LE*, p. 164), which Pound ultimately translated "or delight whereby 'tis called 'to love' " (Ezra Pound, *The Cantos*, p. 177). But in an earlier version, which is the subject of the paragraphs quoted from the essay, he had produced a fantastic line: "What his placation; why he is in verb" (Pound, *LE*, p. 155; Pound, *CSP*, p. 265).

28. Ezra Pound and Marcella Spann, eds., *Confucius to Cummings: An Anthology of Poetry*, p. xi.

29. Ibid., p. 171. (Pound's remarks are clearly indicated as his and not the other editor's.)

30. Ibid., p. 322.

CHAPTER 4

1. Ezra Pound, *Collected Shorter Poems*, p. 46.

2. See Conrad Aiken, "King Bolo and Others," in *T. S. Eliot: A Symposium*, ed. Richard March and Tambimuttu, p. 23.

3. Though the poem seems uncharacteristic, it is identified as Pound's in Donald Gallup, *A Bibliography of Ezra Pound*, p. 397; it is said to be "presumably by Pound" in K. K. Ruthven, *A Guide to Ezra Pound's Personae*, p. 262.

4. Ezra Pound, *Letters, 1907–1941*, p. 15.

5. Ezra Pound, *A Lume Spento and Other Early Poems*, p. 7. The poem by William Carlos Williams referred to is probably "Hic Jacet," in *Collected Earlier Poems*, p. 30. Wardour Street in London, known for its concentration of "dealers in antique and imitation-antique furniture," donated its name to "the pseudo-archaic diction affected by some modern writers" (*OED*, s.v. "Wardour-street"). See also H. W. Fowler, *A Dictionary of Modern English Usage*, corrected ed. (Oxford: Clarendon Press, 1940), pp. 700–701. Fowler's work, begun in 1911 and published first in 1926, is especially useful in the study of Pound's work because Fowler catalogues the stylistic follies prevalent in England at roughly the same time Pound was living there. In *Ezra Pound: His Metric and Poetry* (1917), Eliot cites an anonymous criticism from *Punch*, which noted that "Mr. Ezekiel Ton" evolved "a blend of the imagery of the unfettered West, the vocabulary of Wardour Street, and the sinister abandon of Borgiac Italy"—*To Criticize the Critic* (London, 1965), p. 174.

6. See above, p. 3.

7. Ezra Pound, *The Cantos*, p. 59.

8. Among the jettisoned poems, "Masks" (Pound, *ALS*, p. 52) is interesting for the way it prefigures Pound's repeated use of *Personae* as a title.

9. " 'Time's bitter flood' " (Pound, "In Exitum Cuiusdam," in *CSP*, p. 71) is an ironic quotation from Yeats's "The Lover Pleads with His Friend for Old Friends."

10. I do not want to belabor the significance of relatively insignificant words, but it seems to me that "*the* black panther" is a much stabler expression than "*a* black panther"; the latter carries a potential for mysterious suspense not found in the former, so that the effect of "the" here is to relax the surface of the poem while keeping its substance under tension.

11. In 1916 Pound refers to "Heather" as a kind of writing beyond the poetry of masks:

"I began [my] search for the real in a book called *Personae* [1909], casting off, as it were, complete masks of the self in each poem. I continued in a long series of translations, which were but more elaborate masks.

"Secondly, I made poems like 'The Return,' which is an objective reality and has a complicated sort of significance. . . . Thirdly, I have written 'Heather,' which represents a state of consciousness, or 'implies' or 'implicates' it." Ezra Pound, *Gaudier-Brzeska*, p. 85.

12. The double vertical lines suggest the strongest of the three Gregorian bar notations that indicate the desired phrasing; the weaker notations are the full line and the half line. See Howard Boatwright, *Introduction to the Theory of Music* (London: Peter Owen Ltd., 1956), p. 128. In 1913 Pound said, "M. Henri Martin Barzun has an idea that we should write poems like orchestral scores with a dozen voices at once." Ezra Pound, "The Approach to Paris, Part VII," *New Age* 13 (16 October 1913): 728. In a letter of February 1939 he said of *The Cantos*, "Given time and technique I might even put down the musical notation of passages or 'breaks into song' "; and in October of the same year he used a full line as part of the punctuation of the text of a song. Pound, *Ltrs*, p. 322. See also the *Oxford English Dictionary* (s.v. "Plainsong"), which cites H. B. Briggs's description: "Plain-song or *Cantus planus*—even, level, plain song—is perfectly distinct from *cantus figuratus*, or *mensuratus*, i.e. harmonized, measured music, from which it essentially differs in tonality and rhythm. . . . In plainsong, the accents occur irregularly, thus making the rhythm *free*, but subject to certain laws of proportion which satisfy the ear."

13. See especially the praise for Guido Cavalcanti's treatment of mystical states of mind in Ezra Pound, *Translations*, p. 18. Pound's clearest exposition of his notion of the evolution of myth from intense personal experience is in "Psychology and the Troubadours," in *The Spirit of Romance*, p. 92. See also his claim, "I have seen the God Pan," in an essay on Arnold Dolmetsch, in Ezra Pound, *Literary Essays*, p. 431.

14. Pound's appropriation of the specifically Christian plainsong form recalls his description of the probable practice among troubadours: "If a certain number of people in Provence developed their own unofficial mysticism, basing it for the most part on their own experience, if the servants of Amor saw visions quite as well as the servants of the Roman ecclesiastical hierarchy, if they were, moreover, troubled with no 'dark night of the soul,' and the kindred incommodities of ascetic yoga, this may well have caused some scandal and jealousy to the orthodox. If we find a similar mode of thought in both devotions, we find a like similarity in the secular and sacred music. 'Alba' was probably sung to 'Hallelujah's' melody." Pound, *SR*, p. 91.

15. Pound, *SR*, pp. 153–54.

16. Pound, 'Psychology and Troubadours," p. 87. In 1916 Pound wrote that a collection of five or six Japanese Noh dramas presented in an evening make up a "service" that "presents, or symbolizes, a complete diagram of life and recurrence" and that the Noh has its unity in emotion. "It has also what we may call Unity of Image. At least, the better plays are all built into the intensification of a single Image." In a note Pound added, "This intensification of the Image, this manner of construction, is very interesting to me personally, as an Imagiste, for we Imagistes

knew nothing of these plays when we set out in our own manner. These plays are also an answer to a question that has several times been put to me: 'Could one do a long Imagiste poem, or even a long poem in vers libre?' " Pound, *Translations*, pp. 221–22, 237. One answer came twenty years later when Yeats called *The Cantos* "an immense poem in *vers libre*." William Butler Yeats, ed., *Oxford Book of Modern Verse*, p. xxv.

17. According to Pound's note, the poems in *Cathay* are "for the most part from the Chinese of Rihaku, from the notes of the late Ernest Fenollosa, and the decipherings of the Professors Mori and Ariga" (Pound, *CSP*, p. 136).

18. Donald Davie, complaining about this practice, says, "*Cathay* includes one memorable howler: 'The River Song' is a conglomeration of two distinct poems by Li Po, the title of the second being versified and submerged in the four lines beginning 'And I have moped in the Emperor's garden.' " Donald Davie, *Ezra Pound*, p. 41. The poem, whatever its provenance, seems perfectly unified to me. See also Wai-Lim Yip, *Ezra Pound's Cathay*, pp. 149–53.

19. Pound seems to have been largely indifferent to the real identity of "Rihaku," just as a few years later he expressed indifference to the real name of the "Andreas Divus" who figures in Canto I. See Pound, *LE*, p. 259.

20. A sample of Fenollosa's notes, along with Pound's handling of them, is provided in Noel Stock, ed., *Ezra Pound*, pp. 178–79. See also Hugh Kenner, *The Pound Era*, pp. 192–222, and Wai-Lim Yip, *Ezra Pound's Cathay*.

21. *OED* s.v. "Psychological moment." See also Fowler, *Modern English Usage*, pp. 473–74.

22. Translated by Pound in 1913 or 1914; see Pound, *CSP*, pp. 115–17.

23. Ezra Pound, "Vortex. Pound," *Blast*, no. 1 (20 June 1914), p. 153; quoted in Herbert N. Schneidau, *Ezra Pound*, p. 149.

24. Pound, *Ltrs*, p. 87; see also pp. 55, 91, 218, 295, 296. Producing a list of inventors and masters in "How to Read," Pound says, "I am chucking out Pindar, and Virgil, without the slightest compunction." Pound, *LE*, p. 28.

25. Some critics come to the conclusion that the main poem centers on "E. P." and that Mauberley himself is not considered until the 1920 postscript. The two figures are said to differ in some important ways; Mauberley does not have E.P.'s "half-savage origin or his Capanean intensity." Hugh Witemeyer, *The Poetry of Ezra Pound*, p. 167. See also John J. Espey, *Ezra Pound's Mauberley*, pp. 15–16. A good summary of the opposing points of view is in William V. Spanos, "The Modulating Voice of *Hugh Selwyn Mauberley*," pp. 73–96. A balanced consideration is Walter Sutton, "*Mauberley, The Waste Land*, and the Problem of Unified Form," pp. 15–35.

CHAPTER 5

1. Donald Gallup says, "Cantos LXXII and LXXIII, omitted from the sequence, are being withheld for the time being from publication by the author." Donald Gallup, *A Bibliography of Ezra Pound*, p. 103. Daniel D. Pearlman rejects the idea that the poems have been suppressed because of libelous contents; he says that he has found out from the poet's daughter that these Cantos, dealing with Pound's friends, are written in a style "prelusive of the *Pisan Cantos*." Daniel D. Pearlman, *The Barb*

of Time, p. 234n. But if that is the case, it is hard to see why the poems have not been made public. See also Mary de Rachewiltz, *Discretions*, p. 197, and C. David Heymann, *Ezra Pound*, pp. 153, 335.

2. See Ezra Pound, "Canto Proceeding (72 Circa)," *Vice Versa* 1 (January 1942): 1–2; Ezra Pound, *Drafts & Fragments of Cantos CX–CXVII* (New York, 1969), pp. 28–29. "Sassoon" and "Rothschild" in *Vice Versa* appear as "S......" and "R........" in *D&F*.

3. Ezra Pound, *Letters, 1907–1941*, p. 348.

4. Ezra Pound, *A Lume Spento and Other Early Poems*, p. 87.

5. Ezra Pound, *Selected Cantos*, p. 91.

6. Donald Hall, "The Art of Poetry," p. 23.

7. William Butler Yeats, *A Vision*, pp. 4–5.

8. Cf. "The Cantos contain nothing in the nature of cypher or intended obscurity." Ezra Pound, "A Note to Base Censor," *Paris Review* 28 (Summer–Fall): 17.

9. Ezra Pound, *Guide to Kulchur*, p. 194.

10. Ezra Pound, "An Introduction to the Economic Nature of the United States," in *Impact*, p. 15. This article is a revised version of Carmine Amore's translation of Pound's Italian pamphlet, *Introduzione alla natura economica degli S. U. A.* (1944).

11. See above, p. 121.

12. Lewis Leary, ed., *Motive and Method in the Cantos of Ezra Pound*, p. 52.

13. Ibid., pp. 47–48.

14. Ezra Pound, *A B C of Reading*, p. 89.

15. Ezra Pound, *The Cantos*, p. 6.

16. See above, p. 147.

17. See above, p. 104.

18. Ezra Pound, *The Spirit of Romance*, p. 166.

19. Ibid., pp. 128–29.

20. One error, which might be too large to be a matter of mere detail, is Pound's mistaken assumption that Zaharoff was a Jew; he made the same mistake about Max Beerbohm, obviously the model for "Brennbaum" in *Hugh Selwyn Mauberley*. One remembers, with distress, one of Hemingway's early sketches in which a policeman murders two Hungarian burglars for no good reason and then says, "I can tell wops a mile off."

21. Ezra Pound, *Literary Essays*, p. 154. The "rose" pattern of filings is one of Pound's favorite figures, as in Canto LXXIV: "Hast 'ou seen the rose in the steel dust" (Pound, *C*, p. 449). His earliest use of the figure that I have come across is in one part of a series called "Through Alien Eyes" in 1913: "If you pour a heap of iron filings on to a glass plate they form a heap; no amount of care and thought [would] make you able to arrange them bit by bit in a beautiful manner. Clap a strong enough magnet to the underside of the plate and at once the filings leap into order. They form a rose pattern on the lines of the electric force and they move in unison." *New Age* 12 (16 January 1913): 252. This image of instantaneous organization has provided the titles of two studies of Pound, Walter Baumann's *The Rose in the Steel Dust* and Lore Lenberg's *Rosen aus Feilstaub*. Lest we become lost in the contemplation of this seminal figure of speech, I feel obliged to cite a few remarks on the

subject by a British physicist: "Our acquaintance with magnetism at school is usually first made through the famous experiment in which iron filings are sprinkled over the surface of a magnet laid on a piece of white card, thereby delineating its magnetic lines of force. The impact of this experiment on the pupil's mind is evidently tremendous, for it appears to obliterate the memory of all others. The sum total of magnetism to millions of adults can be adequately summed up in the phrase 'iron filings and all that.'" Eric W. Lee, *Magnetism* (Harmondsworth, Middlesex: Penguin Books, 1963), p. 7.

22. See above, p. 95.

23. Pound, *LE*, pp. 394–96.

24. Ezra Pound, *Collected Shorter Poems*, p. 113. See above, p. 118.

25. Another book that begins with an "and" is the Authorized Version of *The Apocrypha*: "And Josias held the feast of the passover." This is the opening of I Esdras, which, according to various traditions, is either the first or third book of Ezra. It is probably not significant in this regard that Ezra Pound's Canto I was originally a part of Canto III.

26. The Latin is *periplus*; Pound's form is idiosyncratic, as is the meaning he assigns it. A map and a *periplus* are not mutually exclusive. See *OED* s.v. "Periplus."

27. Pound, *CSP*, p. 206.

28. A corollary, "must fight for law as for walls," is identified as "Herakleitos' parenthesis" in Canto XCVIII (Pound, *C*, p. 685). Heracleitus' Fragment 44 is given as "The people should fight for the Law (*Nomos*) as if for their city-wall," in Kathleen Freeman, *Ancilla to the Pre-Socratic Philosophers* (Cambridge, Mass.: Harvard University Press, 1962), p. 27. *Nomos*—formal law—is invoked also at the end of Canto LXXI (Pound, *C*, p. 421).

29. Pound, *Ltrs*, p. 348; Pound, *C*, p. 800. This unusual figure may owe something to Yeats's "Long-legged Fly" or to a passage in Coleridge's *Biographia Literaria*, chapter 7: "Most of my readers will have observed a small water-insect on the surface of rivulets which throws a cinque-spotted shadow fringed with prismatic colours on the sunny bottom of the brook; and will have noticed how the little animal wins its way up against the stream, by alternate pulses of active and passive motion, now resisting the current, and now yielding to it in order to gather strength and a momentary fulcrum for a further propulsion. This is no unapt emblem of the mind's self-experience in the act of thinking."

30. Pound, *C*, pp. 616, 645, 684. See also Hugh Kenner, "Leucothea's Bikini: Mimetic Homage," in *Ezra Pound*, ed. Noel Stock, pp. 25–40.

31. Pound, *SR*, p. 218.

32. The line "Time is not, Time is the evil, beloved" appears in Canto LXXIV (Pound, *C*, p. 444).

33. Pound, *LE*, p. 212.

34. D. D. Pearlman illuminates this passage by relating the source of the inscription (in Ecclesiastes) to a theme of time-as-order in *The Cantos*. Pearlman is wrong, however, in saying that the only other place in which Pound uses the motto is in *Letters*, p. 341. The words recur in Canto LXXIV (Pound, *C*, p. 429); and the dedication to *Selected Cantos* reads, "To Olga Rudge / 'Tempus loquendi.'" See Pearlman, *Barb of Time*, pp. 142–44.

35. For a time after the Second World War, Pound's letterhead was the motto "J'ayme donc je suis" arranged in a semicircle. See facsimile in Julien Cornell, *The Trial of Ezra Pound*, p. 93. Pound's use of mottolike Latin phrases—in "Amo ergo sum" and also in such titles as "Erat Hora," and "Sub Mare," and "Beatae Horae Inscriptio"—gives the impression of permanence; perhaps only a "dead" language can convey such a degree of timelessness.

36. Cornell, *The Trial*, pp. 74–75. Cornell prints facsimiles of several letters, which are scrawled irregularly so that they are rather hard to read. Cornell explains that "Domenica" and "aiuto" are Italian for "Sunday" and "help."

APPENDIX

1. Zeno's paradoxes of motion, for example, "refuted by philosophers for 2400 years," still challenge mathematicians, metaphysicians, and physicists. See Richard M. Gale, ed., *The Philosophy of Time*, p. 387.

2. Gotthold Ephraim Lessing, *Laocoön, Nathan the Wise, and Minna von Barnhelm*, pp. 1–110.

3. See Bernard Weinberg, "Castelvetro's Theory of Poetics," in *Critics and Criticism*, ed. R. S. Crane, pp. 160–65.

4. Lessing, *Laocoön*, p. 55.

5. Augustine *Confessions* 11.

6. The letter, dated 2 January 1810, was addressed to Thomas Manning. Charles Lamb, *The Letters of Charles Lamb*, ed. E. V. Lucas (New Haven: Yale University Press, 1935), 2:90.

7. Jerome Buckley, *The Triumph of Time*. See also J. B. Priestley, *Man and Time*, esp. pp. 106–35.

8. William H. McNeill, *The Rise of the West*, p. 732.

9. McNeill, *Rise of the West*, p. 760.

10. John Dewey, *The Influence of Darwin on Philosophy*, p. 1. Ludwig Wittgenstein, on the other hand, said that "die Darwinsche Theorie hat mit der Philosophie nicht mehr zu schaffen als irgend eine andere Hypothese der Naturwissenschaft." *Tractatus Logico-Philosophicus* (London: Routledge & Kegan Paul, 1961), p. 48. In one place at least, Pound seems to agree with Wittgenstein's position: "In our time Al Einstein scandalized the professing philosophists by saying, with truth, that his theories of relativity had no philosophic bearing." Ezra Pound, *Guide to Kulchur*, p. 34.

11. Samuel Alexander, *Space Time and Deity*, 1:36, 44. See also H. Wildon Carr, " 'Time' and 'History' in Contemporary Philosophy; With Special Reference to Bergson and Croce," *Proceedings of the British Academy*, 1917–18, pp. 331–49.

12. Henri Bergson, *Time and Free Will*, pp. 75–139.

13. Ibid., p. 133.

14. Henri Bergson, *Le Rire*, translated as *Laughter*, in *Comedy*, ed. Wylie Sypher (Garden City, N.Y.: Doubleday & Co., 1956), p. 79.

15. T. E. Hulme, *Speculations*, p. 126.

16. Lewis has much in common with a certain Professor Jones who transforms the names of Bergson and Einstein into "Bitchson" and "Winestain"—coinages suggesting femininity, bestiality, fluidity, and disorder. James Joyce, *Finnegans Wake*, p. 149.

17. Wyndham Lewis, *Time and Western Man*, pp. 54, 67, 85–135. Joyce reciprocated by caricaturing Lewis. Pound, who had praised Lewis earlier (see Ezra Pound, *Literary Essays*, pp. 423–30), was less vindictive than Joyce. He said later with good humor, "Mr. W. Lewis, calling me in one place a revolutionary simpleton, makes

honourable amend, calling himself a chronological idiot in another" (Pound, *GK*, p. 234). In Cantos XCVIII and CII he includes Lewis among writers who "had no ground beneath 'em" and "no ground to stand on"—Ezra Pound, *The Cantos*, pp. 685, 728. Significantly, Pound eulogizes Lewis, who died in 1957, in the fragment of Canto CXV (cited above, p. 178) that stands as Pound's own meditation on time and Western man.

18. Edwin Muir, *The Structure of the Novel*, pp. 62–114.

19. E.g., A. A. Mendilow, *Time and the Novel*; and Margaret Church, *Time and Reality*.

20. The management of the temporal pace and sequence in a novel was called by Henry James "the most interesting question the artist has to consider." The novelist must so control his fiction, according to James, that "the mere procession of items and profiles is not only, for the occasion, superseded, but is, for essential quality almost 'compromised.' " In something like an eschatological pun, James goes on to say, "This eternal time-question is, accordingly, for the novelist, always there and always formidable." Henry James, preface to *Roderick Hudson*, in *The Art of the Novel*, p. 14.

21. Lawrence Durrell, *A Key to Modern British Poetry*, p. 23.

22. Durrell, *A Key*, pp. 28–31.

23. London, 1960; first publ. 1933.

24. Edwin Muir, *Collected Poems*, pp. 39, 48.

25. Lawrence Durrell, *Balthazar* (London: Faber & Faber, 1958), p. 7.

26. Loïc Bouvard, "Conversation with William Faulkner," p. 362.

27. Arthur Miller, *Collected Plays*, pp. 5–6.

28. Norman Mailer, "The Man Who Studied Yoga," in *New Short Novels 2* (New York: Ballantine Books, 1956), p. 29.

29. See Lessing, *Laocoön*, pp. 53–54.

30. "The Chinese Written Character as a Medium for Poetry: 2," ed. Ezra Pound, *Little Review* 6 (October 1919): 58.

31. Joseph Frank, "Spatial Form in Modern Literature," in *The Widening Gyre*, pp. 9–10.

32. Frank, "Spatial Form," pp. 12–13. A paraphrase of Frank's idea by René Wellek and Austin Warren is of little use: "In using the term 'world,' one is using a space term. But 'narrative fiction'—or better, a term like 'story,' calls our attention to time, and a sequence in time. 'Story' comes from 'history': the 'Chronicles of Barsetshire.' Literature is generally to be classed as a time-art (in distinction from painting and sculpture, space-arts); but in a very active way modern poetry (non-narrative poetry) seeks to escape its destiny—to become a contemplative stasis, a 'self-reflexive' pattern; and as Joseph Frank has well shown, the modern art-novel (*Ulysses, Nightwood, Mrs. Dalloway*) has sought to organize itself poetically, i.e. 'self-reflexively.' " René Wellek and Austin Warren, *Theory of Literature*, p. 204. See, *contra*, Benedetto Croce, *Aesthetic*, pp. 4, 5, 115; Susanne K. Langer, *Problems of Art*, pp. 37–41.

33. George Santayana, *The Life of Reason*, 4:46–47.

34. Lessing, *Laocoön*, p. 66.

35. See above, p. 76.

36. Hans Meyerhoff, *Time and Literature*, pp. 16ff.

BIBLIOGRAPHY

Adams, Brooks. *The Law of Civilization and Decay: An Essay on History*. 1896. Reprint. New York: Macmillan Co., 1903.

Alexander, Samuel. *Space Time and Deity: The Gifford Lectures at Glasgow*. London: Macmillan & Co., 1920.

Baumann, Walter, *The Rose in the Steel Dust: An Examination of the Cantos of Ezra Pound*. Coral Gables, Fla.: University of Miami Press, 1970.

Bergman, Herbert. "Ezra Pound and Walt Whitman." *American Literature* 27 (1955): 56–61.

Bergson, Henri. *Time and Free Will: An Essay on the Immediate Data of Consciousness*. Translated by F. L. Pogson. 1910. Reprint. London: Allen and Unwin, 1959.

Bouvard, Loïc. "Conversation with William Faulkner." Translated by Henry Dan Piper. *Modern Fiction Studies* 5 (Winter 1959–60): 361–64.

Buckley, Jerome. *The Triumph of Time: A Study of the Victorian Concepts of Time, History, Progress, and Decadence*. Cambridge, Mass.: Harvard University Press, 1966.

Church, Margaret. *Time and Reality: Studies in Contemporary Fiction*. Chapel Hill: University of North Carolina Press, 1963.

Cornell, Julien. *The Trial of Ezra Pound*. New York: John Day Co., 1966.

Crane, R. S., ed. *Critics and Criticism, Ancient and Modern*. Abridged ed. Chicago: University of Chicago Press, 1957.

153

Croce, Benedetto. *Aesthetic*. Translated by Douglas Ainslie. Originally published as *Aesthetic as Science of Expression and General Linguistic*. 1909. Reprint. New York: Noonday, 1968.

Cummings, E. E. *Complete Poems: 1913–1962*. New York: Harcourt Brace Jovanovich, 1972.

Daniel, Glyn. *The Idea of Prehistory*. London: Cleveland, World, 1964.

Davie, Donald. *Ezra Pound: Poet as Sculptor*. London: Routledge & Kegan Paul, 1965.

de Rachewiltz, Mary. *Discretions*. London: Faber & Faber, 1971.

Dewey, John. *The Influence of Darwin on Philosophy*. New York: Henry Holt & Co., 1910.

Durrell, Lawrence. *A Key to Modern British Poetry*. Norman, Okla.: University of Oklahoma Press, 1964.

Eliot, T. S. *Four Quartets*. New York: Harcourt Brace & Co., 1943.

————. *The Sacred Wood: Essays on Poetry and Criticism*. 1920. Reprint. London: Methuen & Co., 1960.

————. *Selected Essays*. 3rd ed. Reprint. London: Faber & Faber, 1972.

————. *To Criticize the Critic and Other Writings*. London: Faber & Faber, 1965.

Ellmann, Richard. *Eminent Domain: Yeats among Wilde, Joyce, Pound, Eliot, and Auden*. New York: Oxford University Press, 1967.

Espey, John J. *Ezra Pound's Mauberley: A Study in Composition*. Berkeley and Los Angeles: University of California Press, 1955.

Fitts, Dudley. "Music Fit for the Odes." [A review of Ezra Pound's *A Draft of XXX Cantos*] *Hound and Horn* 4 (January–March 1931): 278–89.

Frank, Joseph. *The Widening Gyre: Crisis and Mastery in Modern Literature*. New Brunswick, N.J.: Rutgers University Press, 1963.

Frobenius, Leo. *Paideuma: Umrisse einer Kultur- und Seelenlehre*. 3rd ed. Frankfurt: Frankfurter Societäts-Druckerei, 1928.

Frye, Northrop. *Anatomy of Criticism: Four Essays*. 1957. Reprint. New York: Atheneum Publishers, 1968.

Gale, Richard M., ed. *The Philosophy of Time: A Collection of Essays*. Garden City, N.Y.: Anchor Books, 1967.

Gallup, Donald C. *A Bibliography of Ezra Pound*. London: Hart-Davis, 1963.

————. "T. S. Eliot and Ezra Pound: Collaborators in Letters." *Atlantic*, January 1970, pp. 48–62.

Haberland, Eike, ed. *Leo Frobenius: An Anthology*. Wiesbaden: Steiner, 1973.

Hall, Donald. "The Art of Poetry: 5" [Interview with Pound]. *Paris Review* 28 (Summer-Fall 1962): 22–51.

Harrison, John R. *The Reactionaries: Yeats, Lewis, Pound, Eliot, Lawrence: A Study of the Anti-Democratic Intelligentsia*. New York: Schocken Books, 1967.

Hemingway, Ernest. *A Moveable Feast*. London: Jonathan Cape, 1964.

Hesse, Eva, ed. *New Approaches to Ezra Pound: A Coordinated Investigation of Pound's Poetry and Ideas*. London: Faber & Faber, 1969.

Heymann, C. David. *Ezra Pound: The Last Rower: A Political Profile*. New York: Viking Press, 1976.

Hone, Joseph. *W. B. Yeats: 1865–1939*. New York: Macmillan Co., 1943.

Hulme, T. E. *Speculations: Essays on Humanism and the Philosophy of Art*. Edited by Herbert Read. New York: Harcourt, Brace & Co., 1924.

James, Henry. *The Art of the Novel: Critical Prefaces*. Edited by Richard P. Blackmur. New York: Charles Scribner's Sons, 1934.

Joyce, James. *Finnegans Wake*. New York: Viking Press, 1939.

Kenner, Hugh. *The Pound Era*. Berkeley and Los Angeles: University of California Press, 1971.

Langer, Susanne K. *Philosophy in a New Key*. 3rd ed. Cambridge, Mass.: Harvard University Press, 1957.

————. *Problems of Art*. New York: Scribner, 1957.

Leary, Lewis, ed. *Motive and Method in "The Cantos" of Ezra Pound*. 1954. Reprint. New York: AMS Press, 1969.

Lenberg, Lore. *Rosen aus Feilstaub*. Wiesbaden: Limes, 1966.

Lessing, Gotthold Ephraim. *Laocoön, Nathan the Wise, and Minna von Barnhelm*. Translated by William A. Steel. London: Dent, 1930.

Lewis, Wyndham. *One-Way Song*. 1933. Reprint. London: Methuen & Co., 1960.

————. *Time and Western Man*. London: Chatto, 1927.

March, Richard, and Tambimuttu, eds. *T. S. Eliot: A Symposium*. London: Editions Poetry London, 1948.

McNeill, William H. *The Rise of the West: A History of the Human Community*. Chicago: University of Chicago Press, 1963.

Mendilow, A. A. *Time and the Novel*. London: Nevill, 1952.

Meyerhoff, Hans. *Time in Literature*. Berkeley and Los Angeles: University of California Press, 1955.

Miller, Arthur. *Collected Plays*. New York: Viking Press, 1958.

Muir, Edwin. *Collected Poems*. London: Faber & Faber, 1960.

————. *The Structure of the Novel*. London: Hogarth, 1928.

Olson, Charles. *Selected Writings*. Edited by Robert Creeley. New York: New Directions, 1966.

Patrides, C. A., ed. *Aspects of Time*. Manchester: Manchester University Press, 1976.

Pearce, Roy Harvey, ed. *Whitman: A Collection of Critical Essays*. Twentieth Century Views. Englewood Cliffs, N.J.: Prentice-Hall, 1962.

Pearlman, Daniel D. *The Barb of Time: On the Unity of Ezra Pound's Cantos*. New York: Oxford University Press, 1969.

Pound, Ezra. *A B C of Reading*. 1934. Reprint. Norfolk, Conn.: New Directions, 1951.

————. *A Lume Spento and Other Early Poems*. New York: New Directions, 1965.

————. *Antheil and "The Treatise on Harmony."* Paris: Three Mountains, 1924.

————. *The Cantos*. New York: New Directions, 1970.

————. *Collected Shorter Poems*. London: Faber & Faber, 1968.

———— and Spann, Marcella, eds. *Confucius to Cummings: An Anthology of Poetry*. New York: New Directions, 1964.

————. *Gaudier-Brzeska: A Memoir*. 1916. Reprint. New York: New Directions, 1960.

————. *Guide to Kulchur*. New ed. Norfolk, Conn.: New Directions, 1968.

————. *Impact: Essays on Ignorance and the Decline of American Civilization*. Edited by Noel Stock. Chicago: Henry Regnery Co., 1960.

———— *Jefferson and/or Mussolini*. New York: Liveright, 1936.

———— *Letters, 1907–1941*. Edited by D. D. Paige. New York: Harcourt Brace & Co., 1950.

———— *Literary Essays*. Edited by T. S. Eliot. Reprint. New York: New Directions, 1968.

———— *Make It New: Essays by Ezra Pound*. London: Faber & Faber, 1934.

———— *Patria Mia*. Chicago: Robert F. Seymour, 1950.

———— *Pavannes and Divagations*. Norfolk, Conn.: New Directions, 1958.

———— *Pavannes and Divisions*. New York: Alfred A. Knopf, 1918.

———— *Selected Cantos*. London: Faber & Faber, 1967.

———— *The Spirit of Romance*. Orig. ed. 1910; rev. ed. 1952. Reprint. Norfolk, Conn.: New Directions, 1953.

————. *Translations*. Edited by Hugh Kenner. Norfolk, Conn.: New Directions, 1963.

Priestley, J. B. *Man and Time*. Garden City, N.Y.: Doubleday & Co., 1964.

Quinn, Bernetta. *Ezra Pound: An Introduction to the Poetry*. New York: Columbia University Press, 1972.

Read, Forrest, ed. *Pound/Joyce: The Letters of Ezra Pound to James Joyce, with Pound's Essays on Joyce*. New York: New Directions, 1967.

Russell, Peter, ed. *An Examination of Ezra Pound: A Collection of Essays*. Norfolk, Conn.: New Directions, 1950.

Ruthven, K. K. *A Guide to Ezra Pound's Personae.* Berkeley and Los Angeles: University of California Press, 1969.

Santayana, George. *The Life of Reason.* 5 vols. Vol. 4, *Reason in Art.* New York: Collier Books, 1962.

Schneidau, Herbert N. *Ezra Pound: The Image and the Real.* Baton Rouge: Louisiana State University Press, 1969.

Seelye, Catherine, ed. *Charles Olson and Ezra Pound: An Encounter at St. Elizabeths.* New York: Grossman Pubs., 1975.

Spanos, William V. "The Modulating Voice of *Hugh Selwyn Mauberley.*" *Wisconsin Studies in Contemporary Literature* 6 (Winter-Spring 1965): 73–96.

Stock, Noel, ed. *Ezra Pound Perspectives: Essays in Honor of His Eightieth Birthday.* Chicago: Henry Regnery Co., 1965.

————. *The Life of Ezra Pound.* New York: Avon Books, 1970.

————. *Reading the Cantos: A Study of Meaning in Ezra Pound.* London: Routledge & Kegan Paul, 1967.

Sutton, Walter. "*Mauberley, The Waste Land,* and the Problem of Unified Form." *Contemporary Literature* 9 (Winter 1968): 15–35.

Sypher, Wylie, ed. *Comedy: An Essay on Comedy by George Meredith; Laughter by Henri Bergson.* Garden City, N.Y.: Doubleday & Co., 1956.

Wellek, René and Austin Warren. *Theory of Literature.* New York: Harcourt Brace & Co., 1956.

Williams, William Carlos. *Collected Earlier Poems.* Norfolk, Conn.: New Directions, 1951.

————. *Paterson.* New York: New Directions, 1963.

————. *Selected Essays.* New York: Random House, 1954.

Wilson, Edmund, ed. *The Shock of Recognition: The Development of Literature in the United States Recorded by the Men Who Made It.* 2d ed. New York: Farrar, Straus, and Cudahy, 1955.

Witemeyer, Hugh. *The Poetry of Ezra Pound: Forms and Renewal, 1908–1920.* Berkeley and Los Angeles: University of California Press, 1969.

Yeats, William Butler. *Autobiography: Consisting of "Reveries over Childhood and Youth," "The Trembling of the Veil,"* and *"Dramatis Personae."* New York: Collier Books, 1965.

————, ed. *The Oxford Book of Modern Verse.* New York: Oxford University Press, 1937.

————. *A Vision.* Rev. ed. 1938. Reprint. New York: Macmillan Co., 1956.

Yip, Wai-Lim. *Ezra Pound's Cathay.* Princeton, N.J.: Princeton University Press, 1969.

INDEX